KURT COBAIN

KURT COBAIN
THE LAST INTERVIEW
and OTHER CONVERSATIONS

with an introduction by DANA SPIOTTA

MELVILLE HOUSE
BROOKLYN · LONDON

KURT COBAIN: THE LAST INTERVIEW
AND OTHER CONVERSATIONS

Every reasonable effort has been made to trace the copyright holders for these interviews. The editors and publishers will be glad to receive any information leading to more complete acknowledgments for further printings of this book.

First Melville House printing: September 2022

Melville House Publishing   Suite 2000
46 John Street   and   16/18 Woodford Road
Brooklyn, NY 11201   London E7 0HA

mhpbooks.com
@melvillehouse

ISBN: 978-1-68589-009-4
ISBN: 978-1-68589-010-0 (EBOOK)

Printed in the United States of America
1 3 5 7 9 10 8 6 4 2

A catalog record for this book is available from the Library of Congress.

CONTENTS

vii   **INTRODUCTION BY DANA SPIOTTA**

3   **"I CONSIDER ROCK AND ROLL LIKE MATHEMATICS"**
Interview by Bob Gulla
CD NOW
April 18, 1990

15   **SMITH COLLEGE RADIO INTERVIEW**
Interview by Laura Begley and Anne Filson
WOZQ
April 27, 1990

27   **MY EMBARRASSING INTERVIEW WITH KURT COBAIN**
Interview by Roberto LoRusso
WCHR 97.4 London Ontario
September 20, 1991

39   **"I'LL GO BACK TO PLAYING IN FRONT OF 20 PEOPLE–
IF I'M STILL ENJOYING IT"**
Interview by Jon Savage
Guitar World
July 22, 1993

65   **KURT COBAIN, UNPLUGGED**
Interview by Erica Ehm
Much Music TV
August 10, 1993

85   **COBAIN ON COBAIN**
Interview by Edgar Klüsener
August 10, 1993

119   **SUCCESS DOESN'T SUCK**
Interview by David Fricke
Rolling Stone
January 27, 1994

141   **THE LAST INTERVIEW**
Interview by Chuck Crisafulli
Fender Frontline Magazine
February 11, 1994

INTRODUCTION

DANA SPIOTTA

It is one of the jobs of the young to rail against the failures of the previous generation. You can trace a particular line of concern from Holden Caulfield in 1951 to Nirvana in 1991: phonies, conformists, squares, the establishment, the Man, the mainstream, yuppies, corporate culture, poseurs, fakes, sell-outs. The concern comes down to an ideal of authenticity, with maybe the worst sin being hypocrisy. Capitalism has always absorbed and appropriated dissent and resistance, which is why they have to constantly be reinvented in subculture. Nirvana and Kurt Cobain's version in the 1990s was perhaps an apex, and also when tensions within that concern became unsustainable. Afterward, future critiques would have to be differently conceived.

Cobain, like other kids growing up after Vietnam, after Watergate, after the counterculture, absorbed a jaded, knowing quality. An obsession with irony coexisted with an obsession with authenticity. Satire became ubiquitous: *Mad* magazine (full of "take-offs" ridiculing everything from blockbuster films to TV ads), Wacky Packages (stickers on cards that kids collected that had fake advertisements for joke versions of products) and *Saturday Night Live*, which in 1975, its inaugural year, featured Jerry Rubin, the Yippie, in a fake commercial selling wallpaper with hippie and anti-establishment slogans on it. The joke was that Jerry Rubin had sold out, and somehow his knowingness made it okay, but that cynical stance contained a form of surrender. That version of the left seemed to give up. And in fact, Reagan and Thatcher were just around the corner.

Punk rock offered a giant refusal to that cynicism while still cloaking itself in irony. In 1977 the Sex Pistols released the ironically titled single, "God Save the Queen." Johnny Rotten famously sneered as he asked his audience, "Ever get the feeling you've been cheated?" The sneer insured that the joke was complicated: the Pistols were cheating the audience because they defiantly refused to please, but also that the culture had cheated all of them and left them with a kind of nihilism. There was a lot of spitting going on: gobs at the band and gobs back to the audience. As punk developed, it retained its nihilist refusal, but it also had a more egalitarian side. Lester Bangs wrote about the Clash inviting their fans to share their hotel room with them. They were not arena-rock gods, they were just a garage band. Virtuosity on your instrument was not the point, but being politically virtuous was. And it is this strain of punk purity that carried into the 1980s as a counter to the materialist corporate culture of the Reagan years.

There were always traps contained in that youthful fervor for authenticity: how to identify authenticity, first of all, and then how easily markers of authenticity can become just another pose, full of clichés (the hallmarks of hackery). Kurt Cobain, in these interviews that start in 1990, the year before Nirvana made the big time, and end two months before he died in 1994, had internalized the punk rock of the 1980s in the indie/alternative "underground," and we see him grapple with trying to be true to his punk-rock ethics. But it was impossible: one must have the irony, the ambivalence of not caring, of admitting your own complicity in the system. At the same time, one had to care, and follow very strict rules for not selling out. You had to be like Calvin Johnson, maybe, obscure but respected. Kurt Cobain might have been the last person who believed in punk, and he grew weary navigating these tensions. Besides, there was something art-school and elitist in cultivated obscurity, wasn't there? Punk should not be elite (this is the problem with a subculture often defined by what it is not).

One of my favorite threads of punk ethos perhaps came from the Stooges and was picked up on by the Replacements: proud loser-dom. It was a sly form of anti-capitalism, of resistance to the 1980s worship of avarice and material, amoral success. This is illustrated in the famous Sub Pop T-shirt that said LOSER in all caps and extends to Beck's 1994 hit, "Loser." And we can hear this self-deprecation when Cobain says Nirvana is "lazy" and "illiterate" and would lose an argument about any topic because they "took too much acid and smoked too much pot." This is self-deprecation as liberation and subversion—the bullied kids appropriating the words that once were hurled at them. But it is also a kind of pose, as if they didn't want to get caught caring about anything too much. You can't criticize my songs 'cause I already said I suck and can't play. Like all of these threads, it's complicated. Kurt Cobain may not have been schooled in music or literature, but he was good. He was proud of the albums, if not proud of anything else.

But his humility was also real. After the traumatic divorce of his parents ("the legendary divorce is such a bore" he professed in "Serve the Servants"), he led an itinerant existence, even living in his car sometimes. He was a high school dropout, worked as a janitor, but was mostly unemployed. The thing that saved him, the place he began and finished, was music. He was a true believer in music as a space where he could be himself. He began with total commitment to writing songs, playing his guitar, and performing. And he knew how he wanted the music to sound. He wanted it to be like the music he loved: raw and hard but with pop hooks and lyrics you could hear over and over and still find oddness and interest in them. As much like the Beatles as Black Flag, which turned out to be very appealing to a big audience. The problem was what the world did with the music, with selling the music, and with promoting the music. Ultimately, in his interviews, you can see him trying to work that part of it out. He doesn't want an "image." And, as in his lyrics, he manages sarcasm and ambivalence while also exposing how much he cared, a lot, about everything, and constantly. While this worked in his songs, it was harder to pull off in his life. In interviews, he often lied or obscured while also being almost compulsively honest, vulnerable, a person in pain who kept confessing and pouring his heart out even as he felt betrayed by the press and unnerved by his fans.

He continued to do interviews even after the infamous *Vanity Fair* article that portrayed his relationship with Courtney Love in a cruel, harsh light. He became wary, defensive, angry, yet he still kind of believed that he could break through, regain control. He passionately voiced his complaints. Why didn't he just shut it all out, become a recluse? He must have wanted, on some very deep level, to be understood. He must have believed that he could be understood. He could not be indifferent or ambivalent no matter how he professed it.

He denied he had ambition, but then admitted it. He wanted to make records and have an audience. He just wanted to do it on his terms, like his punk heroes. At first, his terms meant being on an indie label versus a major label. But this felt unsustainable. Nirvana were not some coddled middle-class kids in suburban garages. They were not even vaguely making a living on Sub Pop. And distribution (a now vintage consideration) sucked. Nirvana thought they could stay true to their vision while getting the advantages of a major label. That worked for Sonic Youth, who also signed with Geffen Records and gained just enough success to still maintain their indie cred, but Nirvana instantly became world-wide super-stars selling millions of records, which was hard to reconcile with punk-rock bona fides. Nirvana complained about MTV but wanted to use MTV as much as MTV used them. They complained of playing big stadiums (arena rock, yuck) and the lack of intimacy and connection. But their audiences were too big now. And who exactly was in the audience? Those same kids that used to bully them when they were in high school. Cobain goes back and forth about this new audience: at first, they are not his true fans. They frighten him. Then he tries to control them. After the runaway success of *Nevermind*, he even puts this in the liner notes to *Insecticide*:

> If any of you in any way hate homosexuals, people of different color, or women, please do this one favor for us—leave us the fuck alone! Don't come to our shows and don't buy our records.

And this points to what was probably the most interesting and enduring and new thing about Kurt Cobain's punk ethos. He really wasn't going to be just another rock god, he wasn't going to exploit women, he wasn't going to dog-whistle the cliches of rock and roll masculinity. He was a backwater white boy, but he was not a stereotype, not racist or sexist or homophobic. His sensibility was gay, he declared, and he liked strong, smart women. He was fragile, in constant physical pain, and he admitted it. He was highly married and he didn't date models. He liked being a dad. It even extended to how he looked, or how he presented himself. Like Johnny Rotten, Cobain had great style, but it came out of his own contradictions. He was very pretty, but he didn't comb his hair, and he wore grandpa sweaters. He wore dresses—not sleek glamour man-dresses like Bowie had once worn, but thrift-store cast-offs. And he also wore hospital gowns (his own, which, come on, is really punk). So his style, as it were, came out of his vulnerability, his wearing it all on his sleeve. Or on his T-shirt. He famously wore a T-shirt on the cover of *Rolling Stone* that said CORPORATE MAGAZINES STILL SUCK. (Does that give him cover? No, not really. Is self-reflexivity ever really an out? But it is better than nothing.) He also used his shirts as billboards for other, lesser-known artists. As if to say, if you are all going to stare at me, I might as well use the space for good. He wore a Daniel Johnston T-shirt, and when he was on *MTV Unplugged*, he wore a T-shirt for the proto-riot grrrl band Frightwig. Like REM before him, Nirvana used their fame to promote other artists while also giving credit to their influences (and proving their own cred). Despite MTV wanting the grunge hits and Pearl Jam cameos for Nirvana's *Unplugged* set, Cobain insisted on playing three Meat Puppets songs and having them join the set. He also covered songs he learned from the Vaselines, and Leadbelly, and sang (what was then) a more obscure Bowie track. You could hear devotion in his singing: heart out, heartbroken, heartfelt. He tried to accept his contradictions vis-à-vis MTV, interviews, and his own fans. "Come as you are, as you were, as I want you to be." In his last interview, he said, "I get a few hours to try and subvert the way they view the world." These tensions are never really resolved. They must be lived in. Or through.

In the 2020s, punk is sometimes seen as just another retro "aesthetic," like goth or glam. One pose among many, and it is an expression of sensibility more than ethos. And, of course, artists are expected to pay even more attention to image, marketing, and self-promotion. The always contradictory notion of authenticity is not just quaint, but not even legible. Selling a lot of songs/books/tickets is a sign of quality, and it is fine to do ads, consider yourself a brand, make Marvel movies, etc., because you need to reach people in a noisy world, and you need to make a living if you want to continue being a maker/creator. And there is something refreshing in the lack of pretense about being commodified (not just your work, but you, the maker/creator). Resistance and subculture no longer have to be obscure because there are other values involved beyond the sense of self: virtual communities with horizontal reach that don't need to breakthrough mainstream gatekeepers to be viable. There is the possibility of a real egalitarian leveling of access, which is subversive and anti-corporate. You can take the "sub" out of subculture, or you can say everything is subculture, that there is no mainstream to rail against. Maybe there are just streams: streams of music, of films, and somehow, for some people, streams of revenue. Is it better to be an artist now, or was it better to be stuck on the 120 minutes that MTV allowed late at night for "alternative" music? The answer is, I'm afraid, that it is never a good time to be an artist. But here is 1990s-era Kurt Cobain to tell you that there was something valuable at stake in the struggle to live inside those underlying tensions and contradictions.

KURT COBAIN

"I CONSIDER ROCK AND ROLL LIKE MATHEMATICS"

INTERVIEW BY BOB GULLA
CD NOW
APRIL 18, 1990

BOB GULLA: So, what's your objective as a band?

KURT COBAIN: To write really good music, to write the best music we possibly can. That comes before anything else; it comes before philosophy, image, or playing live. It's always been the main point. Just songs. As a unit we've come a whole lot closer to getting where we wanna be as collaborators.

GULLA: What about attitude, is that important?

KRIST NOVOSELIC:* Attitude? We're a pretty lighthearted bunch.

GULLA: Kurt, you write most of the lyrics . . .

COBAIN: Yeah, but I don't know what they're about. It's more of a lazy thing, you know? We just don't bother cultivating an image. We're definitely opinionated—but we're too illiterate to back up what we have to say. We took too much acid and smoked too much pot to store much information in our

---

* Nirvana's bassist; a high school friend of Cobain's.

brains. So if we were to get into an argument with someone about any topic, we would lose.

GULLA: Did you guys grow up together?

COBAIN: Krist and I grew up in the same town—I guess you could say we "grew up." We spent our late teens together in Aberdeen, Washington, a really secluded place one hundred miles from Seattle. Seattle's considered secluded, but Aberdeen's really isolated.

GULLA: Whatever happened to Jason Everman, your original guitar player?

COBAIN: He had an affair with Krist's father, so we thought it best to kick him out of the band. Yeah, the band got to be a soap opera, so we decided we needed to eradicate the source of all those problems.

GULLA: I'll believe almost anything—but should I believe that?

COBAIN: You don't have to believe it, but you can write it. Krist's father is actually this burly Yugoslavian guy who told Krist at one time that we should trade in our guitars for shovels. He's a fun-loving guy. With Jason, [on the] last tour we drove back home from New York, like fifty hours, and didn't say a word to each other the whole way. The songs we were writing while he was in the band weren't satisfying. He was holding us back. He likes more heavy, slow grunge. Now he's in Soundgarden, and it couldn't have worked out better. It wasn't his fault; we just didn't realize how his tastes ran.

GULLA: Do you enjoy touring?

COBAIN: I wasn't anticipating going on tour, but I'm having a good time. You have to psych yourself up. The drives are pretty long, sometimes twelve or thirteen hours, like the bookers threw a dart at the map to determine where we'd play. But we sleep in, don't show up to sound check if we don't want to. This is what we chose to do, and we always considered rock and roll to be kind of lax. Heck, we may as well not burn ourselves out on it. We're just here to have fun, write songs, and play. We're not trying to climb our way to the top and be popular. We're totally comfortable with the level we're on now. It'd be nice to get a little higher, so we could pay the rent for sure every month. I mean, we just want people to like our music. We don't want a big multimillion-dollar promotional deal to bring us into every high school across the country, to make us into multimillion-dollar paper dolls.

GULLA: If someone came up to you and said, "If you work harder we'll make you rich men," how would you react to that?

COBAIN: We'd have to have a say in everything. We would have to pick our own producer and do the record the way we want. Like Butch Vig. He was right on. My idea of an excellent producer is someone who can take an idea from someone's head and find the best way to put it on tape without their interference. The same with promotion as well. You need someone who's gonna put forth the image that you feel comfortable with. We've gotten a few offers from major labels. They'd call Sub Pop, our label, and ask to talk to us about making us an offer, and Sub Pop told them to fuck off. We don't care about it at all.

GULLA: What happens when all the great indie bands get swallowed up by all the major labels?

COBAIN: Chalk one up for capitalism. Let's get our top hats and tails and have a cigar. Alternative music is no longer alternative once it's in the mainstream.

NOVOSELIC: Something weird's gonna come along, some wave, like bands are gonna wear long, flowing robes, play xylophones, and chant—and it's gonna be hugely popular, and rock and roll will disappear completely . . . Some kind of industrial kazoo music. Rock has come full circle, and it needs to redefine itself or die.

COBAIN: Every band since the mid-eighties has surfaced in a revival act. It's a sure sign that rock is slowly dying. There's nothing like wallowing in the past when everything in the future looks bleak. It happens in every art form. When they're afraid of what's in front of them, they always look back. They'll reach a plateau, and they'll think everything's been done, but in reality they're just not thinking hard enough. They're just stalled. If everybody gives up, though, that's when things start to die.

GULLA: Are you ever afraid that there won't be enough of an audience to listen to alternative music? Your music?

COBAIN: Now that could be circling . . . I don't know who our fans are. Most are like us, it seems, a mixture of white trash and punks who at least appreciate the arts, who may not be . . . I hope it's not the typical thrash-scene metalhead kid who has no clue what we're trying to get at . . . We actually had some jocks at a few of our recent shows, and they liked it a lot. That's scary.

NOVOSELIC: Tonight we're gonna be a zany band, a zany funk-rap-metal band. I'm gonna walk onstage with a Hawaiian shirt, one of those baseball caps that can hold two beer cans and straws that go straight into my mouth. It's gonna be zany. We're gonna do "Louie Louie," "Gloria" . . .

COBAIN: I don't know. I consider rock and roll like mathematics. There's only so much you can do after a while, until someone comes up with an entirely new approach. I mean, we're working with a 4/4-time beat, the standard rock tempo, and there are only so many notes on a guitar.

GULLA: You read all these articles about how bands hate to be branded. Do you feel the same way?

COBAIN: I haven't read too many articles that have tried to do that to us. I see that Soundgarden gets compared to Led Zeppelin so much, it's like, why bother? It's too bad. Someone referred to us in an article once as "Lynyrd Skynyrd without the flares." I thought that was pretty funny—way off, but still pretty funny. [*A waitress delivers food. The band was given forty dollars to eat at a mid-price Cambridge restaurant. Chad Channing* got a calzone.*]

COBAIN: What is that? A pizza all folded up?

CHAD CHANNING: It's baked dough with a bunch of stuff in it.

NOVOSELIC: C'mon, Kurt, eat.

COBAIN: I'm not even hungry. I'm really not, not before a show. I'll just pack it up.

GULLA: So what does money mean to you guys?

COBAIN: We care about paying our rent. You know how it goes. Almost everything we make goes right back into the band. If we didn't abuse our equipment so much, we could probably save a little. I only pay $170 a month, but I shouldn't be saying this 'cause then even more people will want to move to Seattle. We're not gonna work this summer, so we can spend more time at home, write some more songs. The last tour we did in Europe was so bad. We're not going over there again unless we get some guarantees. We worked every night for seven weeks and haven't seen a dime. Plus, we starved; we were only given a budget for one meal a day.

---

* Channing was the band's original drummer. He was replaced in September 1990 by Dave Grohl.

GULLA: Do you guys do much reading on the road?

COBAIN: I get tired of reading real descriptive prose, so I've lately taken to reading everything Charles Bukowski has written. My girlfriend's trying to get me to read Jim Thompson.

NOVOSELIC: My wife and his girlfriend are best friends. They work together in the cafeteria at Boeing. That's good money, man.

GULLA: What are you guys listening to?

COBAIN: Anything that isn't grunge. We listen to Tad, we love all the Sub Pop stuff. Mudhoney's my favorite band. The Fluid, Beat Happening, Young Marble Giants, the Pixies, Lead Belly, John Fahey, Leo Kottke, some bluegrass, Middle Eastern stuff . . .

GULLA: Are you getting tired of the population boom in Seattle?

COBAIN: You know what I wanna see? I wanna see a full-on depression. Just hardship, man. Despair. You know why? People need to get their feet back on the ground. They're so distracted by material things.

NOVOSELIC: They're like: "I can make my car payment, I can make my TV payment, I can afford a nice place to live. In fact, I just redecorated my living room, and I'm paying that off, so things must be all right. I'm pretty happy, and that's all

I care about." But it's junk, just junk. So if we ever got down to a depression, it'll help people find out what real problems are, and that they need to look out for each other instead of stabbing each other in the back to get ahead.

GULLA: I knew you had an attitude—it just took a while to surface.

COBAIN: We shouldn't really be spewing off stuff like that. It's kind of nihilistic; people will start to hate us.

GULLA: What's the best thing about being on the road?

COBAIN: Record-buying . . . Secondhand record stores, to find obscure children's records and old blues records. I really don't go for the CD revolution, either. There's something I like about records. I really can't explain it. I know it sounds stupid, but music to me is kind of sacred. You're supposed to take care of it. If you scratch it up, then heck, you'll have to go out and buy another record. You've ruined something, and if you really like the band, you'll have to go buy it again. I still don't own a CD machine, but some people have given me a few free CDs and now I have to at least deal with it. They do sell well. It's kind of hopeless.

NOVOSELIC: You can't do nothing about nothing. [*Laughs*]

CHANNING: Nothing can be done, so I don't even think about trying. I don't think about the problems of the world. There's no reversing them, so I don't bother trying.

GULLA: So what do you turn your thoughts to?

CHANNING: Fun. That's all I do. I'm just a Joe. Whatever makes anybody happy . . . It's not my business what anyone else wants to do.

COBAIN: That's a better attitude than Krist and I have. We watch the news and get pissed off about it and start spewing on something for days. I usually get intimidated by people who pressure their opinions on me. If I go into a truck stop, I'm gonna get laughed at, or get called "queer," "hippie," or instantly stereotyped. Me, I'm just too sensitive about that kind of stuff to just shake it off. It bothers me too much. Not enough to stay in the house all the time. When I was a kid I thought everything was so great. I was so excited to grow up. But in sixth grade I realized, "Wow, my whole life really sucks. Everyone I know is an asshole."

GULLA: At least you have your music now. What do the new songs sound like?

COBAIN: A few songs sound like the old stuff off of *Bleach*. Some new songs are so mellow that we're probably gonna lose half our audience. Well, maybe. Hopefully, if they're music lovers, they'll like it; if it's good, it's good, right? But there are a couple of acoustic songs, like Leonard Cohen— simple, quiet, manic-depressive songs. They're definitely not commercial. Some of the heavy songs are more raw than the last record. It'll be a mixed bag of songs. I'm real happy about it. We've got to get a meeting together with the record company, get them on the ball, get a little bit better promotion.

GULLA: What will you do after rock and roll?

COBAIN: Hopefully, have enough money to buy a house in the woods. If not, you'd better lock me up, 'cause you never know what'll happen.

SMITH COLLEGE RADIO INTERVIEW

INTERVIEW BY LAURA BEGLEY AND ANNE FILSON
WOZQ
APRIL 27, 1990

WOZQ: What's going on tonight? They won't let you sound check?

COBAIN: Bad organization as usual.

WOZQ: Does this happen to you guys a lot?

COBAIN: Yeah. Seeing bad organization on such a small level makes me realize why the world is so fucked up.

WOZQ: Do you think if you were playing at bigger venues people would be more organized?

COBAIN: No.

WOZQ: You guys are known, actually, as being a "Sub Pop band." What do you think of that?

COBAIN: Well, when someone walks up to me and says, "You're my favorite Sub Pop band," I think, "Jeez, we're your favorite out of five bands? What about the rest of the country?" I don't know. It just scares me. I wonder whether they like us because we're a Sub Pop band or because we're ourselves.

WOZQ: What do you think of the other Sub Pop bands?

COBAIN: I love 'em. It's not like I have to say, "Oh, our label's great. We have good bands." I really like the bands on the label. It isn't because Jon and Bruce [who run Sub Pop] are marketing geniuses. It's because they have good bands on their label. They do a good job of promotion.

WOZQ: I heard they based the whole label on the Motown idea—the regional thing, taking a lot of bands from the same region and marketing them all in one package deal.

COBAIN: It's not as if they've packaged all these bands and told us to all go out there and play fuzz guitar . . .

WOZQ: Were you influenced by each other?

COBAIN: I don't really think so, because most of the bands have been around. They didn't all start up around the same time. I think every Seattle band is just influenced by punk rock. There's always been a good, strong punk rock scene in Seattle. So it's been around for a while.

WOZQ: So, how long have you guys been together as a band?

COBAIN: About three years.

WOZQ: Didn't [Sub Pop] start with Mudhoney?

COBAIN: Mudhoney wasn't actually the first to put out a

record. They just became the most popular because they went on tour with Sonic Youth and they got a lot of exposure.

WOZQ: Were you one of [Sub Pop's] first bands too?

COBAIN: Yeah. In fact, we were together before Mudhoney.

WOZQ: You guys were playing together before Sub Pop even started.

COBAIN: Around that time, when it was just starting up, when they put out the Soundgarden EP. I mean, we definitely didn't have an impact on anyone in Seattle, because we were totally unknown. We'd had a few shows, but we weren't really serious about it. We just decided to record a demo. We didn't even know Sub Pop existed when we did our demo.

WOZQ: Any major label interest?

COBAIN: We don't have any interest in a major label. It would be nice to have better distribution, but anything else that goes on major labels is just a bunch of shit.

WOZQ: Does Nirvana have another album coming out soon?

COBAIN: In September 1990.

WOZQ: Is it already recorded?

COBAIN: We recorded seven songs with Butch Vig, a producer that does Killdozer and a lot of Amphetamine Reptile bands. He's a great guy.

WOZQ: How do you think the album is going to sound?

COBAIN: Well, it doesn't really sound different. We recorded seven songs. There's five that are typically raunchy, heavy Nirvana with even more guitar, and there's two that are manic-depressants. So it's a little bit varied.

WOZQ: The token slow songs . . .

COBAIN: The token reggae song . . .

WOZQ: Any covers on the album?

COBAIN: We don't know. We recorded a Velvet Underground song. The songs will be more poppy sounding.

WOZQ: Trying to get on the radio?

COBAIN: No. Not at all. That has nothing to do with it. I like pop music.

WOZQ: Do you like doing covers?

COBAIN: We made a mistake with "Love Buzz" [on the group's last LP, *Bleach*] because it's our best song as far as I'm concerned. There's nothing worse than when a band does a cover that's better than the original. Basically we took the rim—the bass line—and rewrote that song. We stripped it down.

WOZQ: I thought that song sounded a little bit different than the rest of the stuff on the album.

COBAIN: It's a lot more simple pop.

WOZQ: So, have you guys ever played out here in western Massachusetts before?

COBAIN: I don't know. I'm here in this room. I didn't get to walk around. You see, we don't really get to see the sites. We mainly see the road.

WOZQ: What cities do you like to play?

COBAIN: I'll tell you what cities I *don't* like to play. No, really. The cities I like: San Francisco. Ann Arbor. That's a really great place. People are enthusiastic. They're organized.

WOZQ: Have you been drawing more crowds since the LP was released?

COBAIN: It depends on what city. In some places we're popular. Some places no one has heard of us. It's weird. We don't have much promotion. I can probably count on my hand how many times we've had an interview.

WOZQ: Do you think it's worth it just to play, even if you don't have much of an audience? Do you still enjoy it?

COBAIN: Sure. I like playing just for the hell of it. But not for seven weeks. Playing the same set every night is as boring as a construction job. You get tired of it.

WOZQ: You don't vary the set at all?

COBAIN: We don't have enough songs. We dropped five songs [from *Bleach*] off the set the week after we recorded it. We're not playing them anymore, because they're boring. It's just the same set. Fun, fun, fun. But in Europe we're bigger than breakfast on an underground level.

WOZQ: That's like when Dino[saur] Jr. went to Europe. They got an incredible turnout.

COBAIN: Dino Jr.'s big over there. They accept underground bands over there.

WOZQ: So, what was the deal with Jason Everman [Nirvana's ex-guitarist, now in Soundgarden] last summer?

COBAIN: We kicked him out, 'cause he didn't like to do the songs that we like. He wants to play slow, heavy grunge, and we want to write pop songs.

WOZQ: Are you getting a bit sick of hearing the grunge sound?

COBAIN: Yeah. There's only so much distortion you can take. A lot of bands now are going in different directions and writing different styles of songs. Everyone's experimenting. We don't want to milk the sound as far as we possibly can. The Fluid recorded with Butch Vig in Madison, also. Tad recorded with Steve Albini in Chicago.

WOZQ: Has Nirvana gone through any other band member changes?

COBAIN: No. Just one, and Jason didn't play on the record. He joined the band a week after we recorded it. But we put his name on the record anyway.

WOZQ: Is he from Seattle?

COBAIN: Yeah. He's a really nice guy. We met him maybe a couple of months before we recorded the record, and really liked him, and started hanging out with him. I started thinking that maybe I'd like to do a bit more singing, and didn't want to worry about guitar playing that much. It wasn't a very good idea. We had to practice more.

WOZQ: There's a lot of bands that are doing it with three people.

COBAIN: It's kind of hard. [A fourth person] can help a lot, though. It would be easier to just stand there and sing.

WOZQ: Do you make a concerted effort to jump around on the stage?

COBAIN: Yeah. We choreograph it. There's tape marked all over the floor.

WOZQ: You know, I thought you used to all have long hair. When I saw you guys the last time, I swear all of you had long hair.

COBAIN: Yeah. Hair grows, then you cut it. Kris just shaved his eyebrows and his body. All of us had to stop him.

WOZQ: When I saw him at first, I thought he was one of the security people.

COBAIN: A Nazi. Yeah, he's really into Minor Threat. He just heard it for the first time yesterday. And he's even questioning that.

WOZQ: We saw Fugazi two weeks ago. They played here—a benefit concert for a women's shelter in Northampton. Are you guys into any politically activist movements?

COBAIN: We don't agree with it at all.

WOZQ: How did you spend your Earth Day?

COBAIN: We collected as many plastic and polystyrene goods as we could find and built a big bonfire.

WOZQ: Do you recycle on tour?

COBAIN: Sure do. We throw everything right out the window. Actually, we recycle at home. I think there should be mandatory recycling laws.

WOZQ: But you said you're not into political causes.

COBAIN: Oh, no. Not at all. I don't think it should be related to music. Nobody wants to hear a preacher. If you play guitar, you're supposed to have fun.

WOZQ: That was like at the Fugazi show. It was cool, but Ian MacKaye got up there and lectured to everyone.

COBAIN: I mean, it's fine for some people. But even if we wanted to be politically correct, we couldn't because we're too stupid. We were just a bunch of stoners in high school.

MY EMBARRASSING INTERVIEW WITH KURT COBAIN

INTERVIEW BY ROBERTO LORUSSO
WCHR 97.4 LONDON ONTARIO
SEPTEMBER 20, 1991

Roberto LoRusso interviewed Nirvana for his radio show in London, Ontario. He offers the following caveat for this interview:

This is a terrible interview. I am not feigning self-deprecating modesty when I say this, this is objectively terrible by all journalistic standards. It is so for the following reasons: 1) my questions were poorly crafted because 2) my research was incomplete and inaccurate.

ROBERTO LORUSSO: Yeah, well, what happened is that we've been having a lot of complaints, because we're from a small area in Canada—just down the road, London, Ontario. I don't know if you drove by it on the way up here, or you will when you go down to Detroit. We usually don't have a problem, but we had some complaints recently. I was playing Mr. Bungle, Mike Patton's old band . . .

KURT COBAIN: Yeah, I heard a bit about that.

LORUSSO: Yeah.

COBAIN: Damn.

LORUSSO: And got a bit of shit from my station manager. Not too much. We don't usually have much of a problem with censorship, but there's been a real crackdown in the last little while.

COBAIN: It's happening all over the place.

LORUSSO: Yeah, it's really frustrating. It's just . . . I don't know what to do.

COBAIN: Go start your own pirate radio station.

LORUSSO: Well, that's ultimately what I'm gonna do, because that's what I'm in, right, in school.

COBAIN: Uh-huh.

LORUSSO: So, in the next couple of years, hopefully, I'll learn how to build the sucker.

COBAIN: There are all kinds of manuals and books on the subject.

LORUSSO: Actually, I could have gotten hold of this really low-powered transmitter. I was thinking of souping it up. That would have been right on.

COBAIN: Pretty punk rock! [*Inaudible*]

LORUSSO: Throw it in the back of the van, you know? Right on. Okay, you must excuse this completely contrived inter-view, but, hey. Um, can I get you to do a station ID?

COBAIN: Sure. You're listening to Left-Wing Radio . . .

LORUSSO: 94.7 . . .

COBAIN: 94.7 . . .

LORUSSO: Radio Western . . .

COBAIN: Radio Western, and this is Kurt from Nirvana.

LORUSSO: Cool. Okay, first of all, first question: Why did you decide to start your tour in Toronto?

COBAIN: I think we were planning on starting on the East Coast, so . . . I have no idea. Ask my manager. I didn't even pay attention to the itinerary, where we're going. I mean, I'm glad I'm here, I'm glad we're in Canada. I had no idea that we were even going to come to Canada, really. I mean, I expected to come sometime this year on tour, but I just don't pay atten-tion to the itinerary and where we're going, because—well, I can't say that it's all the same, but it's more exciting that way. Just showing up in a town. I don't really like to pay attention to the politics, or what's been going on in the band, at all. Just be along for the ride.

LORUSSO: You want to distance yourself from all the admin-istrative stuff and just play.

COBAIN: Exactly. That's why we have a manager now; he sets things up for us. Of course, he communicates with Krist, and Krist will tell me basically what's going on. If there's anything we don't like, we'll let them know—it's not like we don't care and we're not listening. They just set up whatever we want and we go along . . .

LORUSSO: You don't really care for doing much in the way of interviews, but that's just—is it because of overkill, or just that you're frustrated with it?

COBAIN: I think it's both. I'm getting really bored with the same questions all the time. It's understandable, and I also realize that most of the interviewers have to ask the standard questions because we don't have much of an image and there's not much of a story behind our band. So what people can grasp, they'll base their interview off of that. But I'm getting really tired of the "independent going onto a major label" stuff. It's happened, and there's nothing we can do about it, so there's no sense in analyzing it, you know?

LORUSSO: Do you feel that going to a major has really brought you a lot more ignorant-interviewer interviews?

COBAIN: Not necessarily. I've realized that a lot of the people we've done interviews with this time around are the same people we've done interviews with before. The same magazines. We've hardly have had any interviews in the States, but I've noticed that more in Europe, where usually they're friends of ours in the first place. It's almost like a little conspiracy:

they're not gonna write shit about us, they're not gonna put us down and make us sound like fools. So it's good in that sense, but it's just getting boring. I don't blame them for asking the same questions.

LORUSSO: Well, are you getting a big push from your label, now that you're on a major?

COBAIN: Yeah, yeah, they're really excited. They're sincerely excited and like the music, they really do.

LORUSSO: It's, like, three-quarters of a million dollars—that's quite a big investment.

COBAIN: Three-quarters of a million dollars? No, we didn't get that much.

LORUSSO: It wasn't that much? That's what I read, it might have been in *M.E.A.T.* magazine. How much was it that you got?

COBAIN: 175,000. 33% tax bracket, 15% to our lawyer, 10% to our manager, $70,000 to Sub Pop, left us with about $20,000 to buy equipment. I don't have a place to live at this moment.

LORUSSO: It's not in your contract? 'Cause John Kastner from the Doughboys, for instance—I know his company pays for his rent. You're not getting that?

COBAIN: We have what was left over from the advance in

a bank account. We have an accountant, and he gives us a little bit of money every month to live. We've been on tour and we've been recording for so long that I haven't had the chance—I got evicted from my apartment about three months ago. Every time we get back, we only have a few days at home, so I usually just go to my mother's. So I haven't found a place to live yet.

LORUSSO: So, you're still struggling?

COBAIN: No, we're not struggling. I think, financially, we're well off. I mean, it's more money than I've ever had in my life. To be able to pay rent every month, it's great, you know? I can't ask for any more.

LORUSSO: You're having fun, then?

COBAIN: Oh yeah, definitely. It's taken a lot of problems away, you know?

LORUSSO: Question about the new album: Why did you choose Butch Vig to produce *Nevermind*?

COBAIN: Because we attempted to record our album about a year and a half ago in Madison, and the demos turned out really well. So we decided to do it again.

LORUSSO: You wanted that Wisconsin sound?

COBAIN: The Wisconsin sound, yeah.

LORUSSO: The lumberjack sound! When you got signed to the new label, did you find any sort of internal pressure to tone your sound down? Or did they pretty much leave it up to you?

COBAIN: No pressure whatsoever. In fact, when we had our first mixes completed, our A & R man said they weren't raw enough. Pretty surprising, but it's true.

LORUSSO: Wow.

COBAIN: Yeah.

LORUSSO: Were you apprehensive at all about signing to Geffen?

COBAIN: Well, with Geffen specifically, no. I mean, we had confidence in them.

LORUSSO: But MCA . . .

COBAIN: A lot of the other labels we were talking to—yeah, I was really worried, because signing away seven years of your life is kind of a major decision.

LORUSSO: Right. I read in *M.E.A.T* magazine—it's a Hamilton- and Toronto-based magazine—that you're a big fan of rap, but dislike white rap groups because, and this is a quote, "The white man has ripped off the black man for long enough." Then how do you feel about Consolidated?

COBAIN: Oh, I don't know, was I drunk at that time? I'm a fan of rap music, but most of it's so misogynistic that I can't even deal with it. I'm really not that much of a fan. I totally respect and love it, because it's one of the only original forms of music that's been introduced. But the white man doing rap is just like watching a white man dance. We can't dance; we can't rap. You know? We may as well just leave it alone.

LORUSSO: Excuse me, I'm Italian. I've got that gene in me, thank you very much.

COBAIN: OK, great, you've had your kneecaps removed at birth!

LORUSSO: [*Laughs*] Any major plans for the future? Another wonderfully vague question!

COBAIN: Uh . . . [*Laughs*]

LORUSSO: Rock and roll lifestyle?

COBAIN: Yeah, whatever, I don't know. Televisions out the window, red snapper, fire extinguishers, sparklers, fireworks . . .

LORUSSO: Screwdrivers, that sort of thing?

COBAIN: Yeah.

LORUSSO: Cool. So, we've been talking to . . .

COBAIN: Kurt from Nirvana.

LORUSO: And you're listening to Radio Western, 94.7 FM in beautiful downtown London, Ontario. I can't get you to do a promo for my show?

COBAIN: Sure, yeah.

LORUSSO: Say who you are, and that you're listening to *Idle Banter*—that's the name of the show, *Idle Banter*.

COBAIN: *Idle Banter?*

LORUSSO: Yeah.

COBAIN: Hi, this is Kurt from Nirvana, and you're listening to *Idle Banter*.

LORUSSO: On 97.4, Radio Western.

"I'LL GO BACK TO PLAYING IN FRONT OF 20 PEOPLE – IF I'M STILL ENJOYING IT"

INTERVIEW BY JON SAVAGE
GUITAR WORLD
JULY 22, 1993

JON SAVAGE: Tell me about your background.

KURT COBAIN: I was born in Aberdeen, Washington, in 1967, and I lived between Aberdeen and Montesano, which was twenty miles away. I moved back and forth between relatives' houses throughout my whole childhood.

SAVAGE: Did your parents split up when you were young?

COBAIN: Yeah, when I was seven.

SAVAGE: Do you remember anything about that?

COBAIN: I remember feeling ashamed, for some reason. I was ashamed of my parents. I couldn't face some of my friends at school anymore, because I desperately wanted to have the classic, you know, typical family. Mother, father. I wanted that security, so I resented my parents for quite a few years because of that.

SAVAGE: Have you made up with them now?

COBAIN: Well, I've always kept a relationship with my mom, because she's always been the more affectionate one. But I hadn't talked to my father for about ten years until last year, when he sought me out backstage at a show we played in Seattle. I was happy to see him because I always wanted him to know that I didn't hate him anymore. On the other hand, I didn't want to encourage our relationship, because I just didn't have anything to say to him. My father is incapable of showing much affection, or even of carrying on a conversation. I didn't want to have a relationship with him just because he's my blood relative. It would bore me.

So the last time I saw him, I expressed that to him and made it really clear that I just didn't want anything to do with him anymore. But it was a relief on both our parts, you know? Because for some years he felt that I really hated his guts.

SAVAGE: You can't duck it.

COBAIN: That's what I've done all my life, though. I've always quit jobs without telling the employer that I was quitting; I just wouldn't show up one day. I was the same in high school—I quit with only two months to go. I've always copped out of things, so to face up to my father—although he chose to seek me out—was a nice relief.

SAVAGE: Have you written about this stuff at all? The lyrics on "Serve the Servants" sound autobiographical.

COBAIN: Yeah. It's the first time I've ever really dealt with parental issues. I've hardly ever written anything that obviously personal.

SAVAGE: What was it like for you growing up?

COBAIN: I was very isolated. I had a really good childhood, until the divorce. Then, all of a sudden, my whole world changed. I became antisocial. I started to understand the reality of my surroundings, which didn't have a lot to offer. Aberdeen was such a small town, and I couldn't find any friends that I was very fond of, or who were compatible with me, or liked to do the things that I liked. I liked to do artistic things and listen to music.

SAVAGE: What did you listen to then?

COBAIN: Whatever I could get ahold of. My aunts would give me Beatles records, so for the most part it was just the Beatles, and every once in a while, if I was lucky, I was able to buy a single.

SAVAGE: Did you like the Beatles?

COBAIN: Oh, yeah. My mother always tried to keep a little bit of British culture in our family. We'd drink tea all the time! I never really knew about my ancestors until this year, when I learned that the name Cobain was Irish. My parents had never bothered to find that stuff out. I found out by looking through phone books throughout America for names that were similar to mine. I couldn't find any Cobains at all, so I started calling Coburns. I found this one lady in San Francisco who had been researching our family history for years.

SAVAGE: So it was Coburn?

COBAIN: Actually it was Cobain, but the Coburns screwed it up when they came over. They came from County Cork, which is a really weird coincidence, because when we toured Ireland, we played in Cork and the entire day I walked around in a daze. I'd never felt more spiritual in my life. It was the weirdest feeling and—I have a friend who was with me who could testify to this—I was almost in tears the whole day. Since that tour, which was about two years ago, I've had a sense that I was from Ireland.

SAVAGE: Tell me about your high school experience. Were people unpleasant to you?

COBAIN: I was a scapegoat, but not in the sense that people picked on me all the time. They didn't pick on me or beat me up, because I was already so withdrawn by that time. I was so antisocial that I was almost insane. I felt so different and so crazy that people just left me alone. I wouldn't have been surprised if they had voted me Most Likely To Kill Everyone at a High School Dance.

SAVAGE: Can you now understand how some people become so alienated that they become violent?

COBAIN: Yeah, I can definitely see how a person's mental state could deteriorate to the point where they would do that. I've gotten to the point where I've fantasized about it, but I'm sure I would opt to kill myself first. But still, I've always loved revenge movies about high school dances, stuff like *Carrie*.

SAVAGE: When did you first hear punk rock?

COBAIN: Probably '84. I keep trying to get this story right, chronologically, and I just can't. My first exposure to punk rock came when *Creem* started covering the Sex Pistols' US tour. I would read about them and just fantasize about how amazing it would be to hear their music and to be a part of it. But I was, like, eleven years old, and I couldn't possibly have followed them on the tour. The thought of just going to Seattle, which was only two hundred miles away, was impossible. My parents took me to Seattle probably three times in my life, from what I can remember, and those were on family trips.

After that, I was always trying to find punk rock, but of course they didn't have it in our record shop in Aberdeen. The first punk rock I was able to buy was probably Devo and Oingo Boingo and stuff like that; that stuff finally leaked into Aberdeen many years after the fact.

Then, finally, in 1984 a friend of mine named Buzz Osborne [singer/guitarist for the Melvins] made me a couple of compilation tapes with Black Flag and Flipper—everything, all the most popular punk rock bands—and I was completely blown away. I'd finally found my calling. That very same day, I cut my hair short. I would lip-sync to those tapes. I played them every day, and it was the greatest thing. I'd already been playing guitar by then for a couple of years, and I was trying to play my own style of punk rock, or what I imagined that it was. I knew it was fast and had a lot of distortion.

Punk expressed the way I felt socially and politically. There were so many things going on at once. It expressed the anger that I felt, the alienation. It also helped open my eyes to what I didn't like about metal bands like Aerosmith and Led Zeppelin. While I really did enjoy, and still do enjoy, some of the melodies those bands have written, I suddenly realized I didn't like their sexist attitudes—the way that they just wrote about their dicks and having sex. That stuff bored me.

SAVAGE: When did you start to think about sexism? Was it an outgrowth of your interest in punk?

COBAIN: No, it was before that. I could never find any good male friends, so I ended up hanging out with the girls a lot, and I just felt that they weren't being treated equally and they weren't treated with respect. I hated the way Aberdeen treated women in general; they were just totally oppressed. The words "bitch" and "cunt" were totally common; you'd hear them all the time. But it took me many years after the fact to realize those were the things that were bothering me. I was just starting to understand what was pissing me off so much, and in the last couple of years of high school I found punk rock and it all came together. I finally understood that I wasn't retarded, you know?

SAVAGE: Did you ever have problems with people thinking you were gay?

COBAIN: Yeah. Even I thought that I was gay. Although I never experimented with it, I thought that might be the solution to my problem. I had a gay friend, and that was the only time that I ever experienced real confrontation from people. Like I said, for so many years they were basically afraid of me, but when I started hanging out with this guy, Myer Loftin, who was known to be gay, they started giving me a lot of shit, trying to beat me up and stuff. Then my mother wouldn't allow me to be friends with him anymore, because she's homophobic.

SAVAGE: So did you stop?

COBAIN: Yeah. It was real devastating, because finally I'd found a male friend who I could actually talk to and be affectionate with, and I was told I couldn't hang out with him anymore. Around that same time, I was putting all the pieces of the puzzle together. He played a big role in that.

SAVAGE: Your lyrics contain some provocative gay references—in particular the line "Everyone is gay," from "All Apologies." Is that a reflection of that time?

COBAIN: I wouldn't say it was a reflection of that time. I'm just carrying on with my beliefs now. I guess it is [provocative] in a commercial sense, because of how many albums we've sold.

SAVAGE: It's very unusual to find bands talking about those kinds of things, particularly in the format that you're using, which is male rock.

COBAIN: Yeah. But I think it's getting better, though, now that "alternative music" is finally getting accepted, although that's a pretty sad term as far as I'm concerned. But at least the consciousness is there, and that's really healthy for the younger generation.

SAVAGE: Have you had any problems from the industry or fans because of your gay references?

COBAIN: Never. Pansy Division covered "Teen Spirit" and reworked the words to "Smells Like Queer Spirit," and thanked us in the liner notes. I think it said, "Thank you to Nirvana for taking the most pro-gay stance of any commercially successful rock band." That was a real flattering thing. It's just that it's nothing new to any of my friends, because of the music we've been listening to for the last fifteen years.

I suppose things are different now. If you watch MTV, they have these "Free Your Mind" segments in the news hour, where they report on gay issues and stuff like that. Pretty much in subtle ways, they remind everyone how sexist the wave of heavy metal was throughout the entire eighties, because all that stuff is almost completely dead. It's dying fast. I find it really funny to see a lot of those groups, like Poison—not even Poison, but Warrant and Skid Row, bands like that—desperately clinging to their old identities, but now trying to have an alternative angle in their music. It gives me a small thrill to know that I've helped, in a small way, to get rid of these people—or maybe at least to make them think about what they've done in the past ten years. Nothing has changed, really, except for bands like Soul Asylum, who've been around for, like, twelve years, have been struggling in bars forever, and now have their pretty faces on MTV. Still, they have a better attitude than the metal people. I think it's healthier. I'd much rather have that than the old stuff.

SAVAGE: The track that first got me into Nirvana was "On a Plain." But what's it about?

COBAIN: Classic alienation, I guess. Every time I go through those songs, I have to change my story because I'm as lost as anyone else. For the most part, I write songs from pieces of poetry thrown together. When I write poetry it's not thematic at all. I have plenty of notebooks, and when it comes to writing lyrics I just steal from my poems.

SAVAGE: Is that how the songs on *In Utero* were written?

COBAIN: A little less so. There are more songs on this album that are thematic, that are actually about something, rather than just pieces of poetry. Like, "Scentless Apprentice" is about the book *Perfume,* by Patrick Süskind. I don't think that I've ever written a song based on a book before.

SAVAGE: Did you read much when you were a kid?

COBAIN: I was probably about fourteen. Junior high. I never took it very seriously. I've never kept personal journals, either. I've never kept a diary, and I've tried to write stories in poetry; it's always been abstract.

The plan for my life, ever since I can remember, was to be a commercial artist. My mother gave me a lot of support in being artistic—she really complimented my drawings and paintings. So I was always building up to that. By the time I was in ninth grade, I was taking three commercial art classes and planning to go to art school. My art teacher would enter my paintings and stuff in contests. But, ultimately, I wasn't interested in that at all, really; it wasn't what I wanted to do. I knew my limitations. However, I really enjoyed art and still like to paint.

I've always felt the same about writing, as well. I know I'm not educated enough to really write something that I would enjoy on the level that I would like to read.

SAVAGE: When did you first visit England?

COBAIN: '89.

SAVAGE: Did you enjoy it?

COBAIN: Yeah. Especially the first time. We also went through the rest of Europe, but by the seventh week I was ready to die. We were touring with Tad. It was eleven people in a really small Volvo van, with all our equipment.

SAVAGE: You mean twelve, with Tad . . .

COBAIN: Fifteen! Depending on whether his stomach was empty or not. He vomited a lot on that tour.

SAVAGE: When did you first realize that things were starting to break for the band?

COBAIN: Probably while we were on tour in Europe in '91. We'd finished the "Teen Spirit" video, and they started to play it while we were on tour. I got reports every once in a while from friends of mine, telling me that I was famous. So it didn't affect me until probably three months after we'd been famous in America.

SAVAGE: Was there one moment when you walked into it and you suddenly realized?

COBAIN: Yeah. When I got home. A friend of mine made a compilation of all the news stories about our band that appeared on MTV and local news programs and stuff. It was frightening. It scared me.

SAVAGE: How long did it scare you?

COBAIN: For about a year and a half—up until the last eight months or so. Until my child was born, I would say. That's when I finally decided to crawl out of my shell and accept it. There were times when I wanted to break up the band because the pressure was so intense, but because I like this band, I felt like I had a responsibility not to.

SAVAGE: Was that around the time of your summer 1992 European tour?

COBAIN: Yes. That was when the band started to really fail me emotionally. A lot of it had to do with the fact that we were playing these outdoor festivals in the daytime. There's nothing more boring than doing that. The audiences are massive, and none of them care what band is on the stage. I was just getting over my drug addiction, or trying to battle that, and it was just too much. For the rest of the year I kept going back and forth between wanting to quit and wanting to change our name. But because I still really enjoy playing with Krist and Dave, I couldn't see us splitting up because of the pressures of success. It's just pathetic, you know? To have to do something like that.

It's weird. I don't know if, when we play live, there is much of a conscious connection between Krist and Dave and I. I don't usually even notice them; I'm in my own world. On the other hand, I'm not saying it doesn't matter whether they are there or not, that I could hire studio musicians or something.

SAVAGE: I know it wouldn't be the same. For me, the original band is you and Krist and Dave.

COBAIN: I consider that the original band too, because it was the first time we had a competent drummer. And for some reason I've needed a good, solid drummer. There are loads of bands I love that have terrible drummers, but a terrible drummer wasn't right for this music. At least, it isn't right for the music that we've written so far.

SAVAGE: You haven't really been on the road for a year, not since the *Nevermind* tour.

COBAIN: I've been recuperating.

SAVAGE: Why did drugs happen? Were they just around?

COBAIN: I had done heroin for about a year, off and on. I've had this stomach condition for, like, five years. There were times, especially during touring, when I just felt like a drug addict—even though I wasn't—because I was starving [a consequence of his condition] and couldn't find out what was wrong with me. I tried everything I could think of. Change of diet, pills, everything . . . exercise, stopped drinking, stopped smoking—and nothing worked. I just decided that if I'm going to feel like a junkie every fucking morning and be vomiting every day, then I may as well take a substance that kills the pain. I can't say that's the main reason why I did it, but it has a lot to do with it. It has a lot more to do with it than most people think.

SAVAGE: Did you find out what the stomach thing was?

COBAIN: No.

SAVAGE: Do you still get it?

COBAIN: Every once in a while. But for some reason it's just gone away. I think it's a psychosomatic thing. My mom had it for a few years when she was in her early twenties, and eventually it went away. She was in the hospital all the time because of it.

SAVAGE: Are you feeling a bit better now?

COBAIN: Yeah. Especially in the last year, since I've been married and had a child, my mental and physical states have improved almost 100 percent. I'm really excited about touring again. I haven't felt this optimistic since right before my parents' divorce.

SAVAGE: Did you find it disheartening that you'd started this band, and you were playing these great songs, when suddenly all this weird stuff started happening in the media?

COBAIN: Oh yeah, it affected me to the point of wanting to break up the band all the time.

SAVAGE: Was it mainly the *Vanity Fair* article? [The September 1992 issue of *Vanity Fair* insinuated that Cobain's wife, Courtney Love, was on heroin during her pregnancy with their daughter, Frances.]

COBAIN: That started it. There were probably fifty more articles based on the story. I'd never paid attention to the mainstream press or media before, so I wasn't aware of people being attacked and crucified on that level. I can't help but feel that we've been a scapegoat, in a way. I have a lot of animosity toward journalists and the press in general. Because it's happening to me, of course, I'm probably exaggerating it, but I can't think of another example of a current band that's had more negative articles written about them.

SAVAGE: Why do you think that is?

COBAIN: A lot of it is just simple sexism. Courtney is my wife, and people could not accept the fact that I'm in love, and that I could be happy. Because she's such a powerful person and such a threatening person, every sexist within the industry just joined forces and decided to string us up.

SAVAGE: Let's talk about *In Utero*. It sounds claustrophobic to me.

COBAIN: I think so, yeah. The main reason we recorded the new album, *In Utero*, with [producer] Steve Albini is that he is able to get a sound that sounds like the band is in a room no bigger than the one we're in now. *In Utero* doesn't sound like it was recorded in a hall, or that it's trying to sound larger than life. It's very in-your-face and real.

Technically, I've learned that the way to achieve that is to use a lot of microphones. I've known that for years, ever since I started recording, because microphones are so directional that if you want ambient sound you need to use a lot of tracks. Or you need to use an omnidirectional microphone, farther away from the instruments, so you can pick up the reverberation from the walls.

SAVAGE: How many mikes did you use for *In Utero*?

COBAIN: I have no idea, but a lot. We had big, old German microphones taped to the floor and the ceiling and the walls—all over the place. I've been trying to get producers to do this ever since we started recording. I don't know anything about recording, but it just seems so obvious to me that that is what you need to do. I tried to get [*Nevermind* producer] Butch Vig to do it, I tried to get [Sub Pop producer] Jack Endino to do it, and everyone's response was, "That isn't how you record." Steve Albini proved it to me on these songs, although I don't know exactly how he did it; I just knew that it had to be done that way. He had to have used a bunch of microphones. It's as simple as that. Which is why live recordings of punk shows sound so good. You really get a feel of what is going on.

SAVAGE: Did you re-record any of the tracks?

COBAIN: No. We remixed a couple because the vocals weren't loud enough. Steve is a good recording engineer but terrible at mixing, as far as I'm concerned. To me, mixing is like doing a crossword puzzle or something. It's like math, or something really technical. It drains you; you really have to concentrate on it. There are so many variations in the tones of each instrument that it can take days to mix a song if you really want to get anal about it. I'm all just for recording and, however it comes out on a tape, that's how it should come out. But for some songs it just doesn't work.

SAVAGE: I really like the slow songs on *In Utero*.

COBAIN: They came out really good, and Steve Albini's recording technique really served those songs well; you can really hear the ambience in those songs. It was perfect for them. But for "All Apologies" and "Heart-Shaped Box" we needed more. My main complaint was that the vocals weren't loud enough. In every Albini mix I've ever heard, the vocals are always too quiet. That's just the way he likes things, and he's a real difficult person to persuade otherwise. I mean, he was trying to mix each tune within an hour, which is just not how the songs work. It was for a few songs, but not all of them. You should be able to do a few different mixes and pick the best. I never thought I would enjoy talking about the technical side of recording. It never made any sense to me before. But now, I don't think it's a bad thing to talk about.

SAVAGE: You appear to be in a really good position, since even if the album doesn't do well you've made the record that you wanted to make.

COBAIN: Absolutely. Oh man, that's why I'm so excited about this record. I actually want to promote this record, not for the sake of selling records but because I'm more proud of this record than anything I've ever done. We've finally achieved the sound that I've been hearing in my head forever.

SAVAGE: You didn't on *Nevermind*?

COBAIN: Not at all. It's too slick. I don't listen to records like that at home. I can't listen to that record. I like a lot of the songs, I really like playing some of them live. In a commercial sense I think it's a really good record, I have to admit that, but that's in a Cheap Trick kind of way. But for my personal listening pleasure, you know, it's just too slick.

SAVAGE: How do you sing? Because you use a number of voices . . .

COBAIN: Most of the time I sing right from my stomach. Right from where my stomach pain is.

SAVAGE: That's where the pain and anger comes from?

COBAIN: It's definitely there. Every time I've had an endoscope, they find a red irritation in my stomach. But it's psychosomatic; It's all from anger. And screaming. My body is damaged from music in two ways: not only has my stomach inflamed from irritation, but I have scoliosis. I had minor scoliosis in junior high, and since I've been playing the guitar ever since, the weight of the guitar has made my back grow in this curvature. So when I stand, everything is sideways. It's weird.

SAVAGE: You could get it sorted out.

COBAIN: I go to a chiropractor every once in a while. You can't really correct scoliosis, because it's a growth of the spine. Your spine grows throughout your adolescent years in a curvature. Most people have a small curvature in their spine anyhow, though some people have to wear metal braces. It gives me back pain all the time. That really adds to the pain in our music. It really does. I'm kinda grateful for it.

SAVAGE: Do you feel now that there are contradictions between your ideals and your enormous success? Is that something that worries you?

COBAIN: I don't really know anymore. I think I was probably feeling a lot more contradictory a year and a half ago, because I was blindly fighting and not even knowing what I was fighting for. And, to a point, I still am. Like I said, I don't really know how to deal with the media. A year ago, I said there was absolutely no fucking way that I would ever speak in public again, and that I would go out of my way to never show my face again. But then I decided that I wasn't going to let a handful of evil journalists dictate my fucking life.

I'm just grateful that within the last year I've come across a few people who happen to be journalists that I trust and I like to talk to.

SAVAGE: Maybe this would be a good time to address some of the rumors that have plagued you. When *Nevermind* hit, there were reports that you were a narcoleptic.

COBAIN: No, no. That was just a story I made up to explain why I slept so much. I used to find myself sleeping a lot before shows. A lot of times the backstage area is such a gross scene, I don't want to talk to anybody. So I just fall asleep. There are so many people that we know now, so many friends and stuff, that I can't ask them to leave. I don't want to act like Axl Rose and have my own bus or my own back room area.

SAVAGE: Speaking of Axl, what is the story behind your altercation with him backstage at the 1992 MTV Video Music Awards?

COBAIN: Well, apparently Axl was in a really bad mood. Something set him off, probably just minutes before our encounter with him. We were in the food tent, and I was holding my daughter, Frances, and he came strutting by with five of his huge bodyguards and a person with a movie camera. Courtney jokingly screamed at him, "Axl, will you be the godfather of our child?" Everyone laughed. We had a few friends around us, and he just stopped dead in his tracks and started screaming these abusive words at us. He told me I should shut my bitch up, so I looked at Courtney and said, "Shut up, bitch, heh!" Everyone started howling with laughter and Axl just kind of blushed and went away. Afterward, we heard that Duff [McKagan, the bassist for Guns N' Roses] wanted to beat Krist up.

SAVAGE: I thought it was great when Krist hit his head with the guitar at the end of your performance that evening. You're all trying to be cool and smashing your instruments, and he really fucked it up—it's really good!

COBAIN: That's happened so many times.

SAVAGE: An impressive finale, and you end up looking really stupid, but that's great too.

COBAIN: It was so expected, you know? Should we just walk off stage, or should we break our equipment again? We went through so many emotions that day, because up until just minutes before we played, we weren't sure we were going to go on. We wanted to play "Rape Me," and MTV wouldn't let us. They were going to replace us if we didn't play "Teen Spirit." We compromised and ended up playing "Lithium." I spat on Axl's keyboards when we were sitting on the stage. It was either that or beat him up. We're down on this platform that brought us up hydraulically, you know? I saw his piano there, and I just had to take this opportunity and spit big goobers all over his keyboards. I hope he didn't get it off in time.

SAVAGE: Tell me, I have to ask what happened with the gun thing. Was all that bullshit? [On June 4, 1993, police arrived at the Cobain home after being summoned to break up a domestic dispute. Love told the officers that they had been arguing over guns in the house.]

COBAIN: Oh, yeah. Total bullshit. That's another thing that just made me want to give up. I never choked my wife, but every report, even *Rolling Stone*, said that I did. Courtney was wearing a choker. I ripped it off her, and it turned out on the police report that I choked her. We weren't even fighting. We weren't even arguing, we were playing music too loud, and the neighbors complained and called the police on us. It was the first time that they had ever complained, and we've been practicing in the house for a long time.

SAVAGE: That's the way they expect you to behave because you're a controversial rock star.

COBAIN: The police were really nice about it, though. I couldn't believe it. See, there's this new law, which was passed that month in Seattle, that says when there's a domestic violence call, they have to take one party or the other to jail. So the only argument Courtney and I got into was who was going to go to jail for a few hours. And they asked us out of the blue, "Are there any guns in the house?" I said no, because I didn't want them to know that there *were* guns in the house. I have an M16 and two handguns. They're put away, there are no bullets in them, they're up in the closet, and they took them away. I can get them back now. I haven't bothered to get them back yet, but it was all just a ridiculous little situation. It was nothing. And it's been blown out of proportion. It's just like I feel like people don't believe me. Like I'm a pathological liar. I'm constantly defending myself. People still haven't evolved enough to question anything that's printed. I'm really bad at that, too. I still don't believe lots of things that I read.

SAVAGE: But you must behave badly sometimes.

COBAIN: Sure. Courtney and I fight. We argue a lot. But I've never choked my wife. It's an awful fucking thing to be printed, to be thought of you. You know, we haven't had any problems, any bad reports, any negative articles written about us in a long time. We thought we were finally over it—that our curse had worn itself out.

SAVAGE: It must also be because people have perceived you as a threat.

COBAIN: I think Courtney is more of a threat than I am.

SAVAGE: What have been the worst temptations engendered by your success?

COBAIN: Nothing I can think of, except Lollapalooza. They offered us a guarantee of, like, six million dollars, and that's way more money than . . . We're going to break even on this tour because we're playing theaters, and the production is so expensive at this level. But other than that, I've never thought of the Guns N' Roses, Metallica, and U2 offers as any kind of legitimate offer. They just never were a reality to me.

SAVAGE: So what are the plans for *In Utero*? How much are you touring to promote it?

COBAIN: We'll tour for about six weeks in the States, starting in October. Then I don't want to commit to anything until we see how I feel physically after that. Maybe we'll go to Europe. I'm sure we'll be over in Europe to support this record within a year, but I'm not sure when. I don't want to set a whole year's worth of touring up.

SAVAGE: There seems to be a tension, in that you're defined as being influenced by punk, and part of punk was that it wasn't cool to be successful. Did you feel that tension, and has it caused you problems?

COBAIN: That's not how I perceived early punk. I thought that the Sex Pistols wanted to rule the world, and I was rooting for them. But then American punk rock in the mid-'80s became totally stagnant and elitist. It was a big turnoff for me. I didn't like that at all. But at the same time, I had been thinking that way for so long that it was really hard for me to come to terms with success. But I don't care about it now.

There's nothing I can do about it. I'm not going to put out a shitty record on purpose. That would be ridiculous. But I would probably have done that a year and a half ago—I would have gone out of my way to make sure that the new album was even noisier than it is. I know we're not going to have the fringe—millions who don't enjoy music, who aren't into our band for any reason other than as a tool to fuck. But we did this record the way we wanted to. I'm glad about that.

SAVAGE: It worried me a bit that you might get into the trap, because it's not interesting.

COBAIN: That defeats the whole reason for making music. I've been validated far beyond anything. But I would gladly go back to the point of selling out the Vogue in Seattle, which holds about three hundred people. I'll gladly go back to playing in front of twenty people—if I'm still enjoying it.

KURT COBAIN, UNPLUGGED

INTERVIEW BY ERICA EHM
MUCH MUSIC TV
AUGUST 10, 1993

ERICA EHM: So I do a book show on Much [the Canadian cable television station MuchMusic].

KURT COBAIN: You do what?

EHM: A book show.

COBAIN: Oh.

EHM: Where I talk to different people about fave books that you've read, and how it's inspired you, or what you learned from it, or something like that. So, do you have a book that comes back to you every once in a while?

COBAIN: Yeah, well, I've read *Perfume*, by Patrick Süskind, about ten times in my life, and I can't stop reading it. It's like something that's just stationary in my pocket all the time, it just doesn't leave me. And every time I'm bored, like I'm on an airplane or something, I read it over and over again—'cause I'm a hypochondriac and it just affects me, makes me wanna cut my nose off.

EHM: What's the book about?

COBAIN: It's about this perfume apprentice in France at the turn of the century, and he is disgusted, basically, with all humans, and he just can't get away from humans. So he goes on this trek, this walk of death, where he goes into the rural areas where there's woods all over the place and there's small villages. And he only travels by night, and every time he smells human, like a fire from a far off way, he'll get really disgusted, hide, and he just tries to stay away from people. I can relate to that. [*Laughs*]

EHM: Do you ever use what you read in any of your songs?

COBAIN: As a matter of fact, I used that very story in "Scentless Apprentice." Yeah. So that's really one of the first times that I've ever used an actual story in a book as an example of a song. I've always tried to stay away from that, but now that I'm running out of ideas more and more, I tend to do that.

EHM: Is it hard when you spend your whole life doing the first few albums and then suddenly everybody needs your attention—you have to do interviews, you have to travel around—then suddenly it's . . . is it hard to come up with ideas?

COBAIN: Mmm, I don't know. I've noticed that people expect more of a thematic angle with our music. They always want to read into it. And before I was just using pieces of poetry and just garbage, you know, just stuff that would spew out of me at the time. And a lot of times when I write lyrics, it's just at the last second, 'cause I'm really lazy. And then I find myself having to come up with explanations for it. So I thought

I'd prevent that this time, and actually have an explanation—
for some of the songs, at least.

EHM: There's a lot of baby references in all the songs. I didn't
think there would be, but you have, like, wombs, babies, baby's breath, baby throw-up . . .

COBAIN: Baby throw-up?! [*Laughs*] I think she's lying . . .

EHM: There's babies everywhere; this has obviously become a
huge part of your life!

COBAIN: It has been a part of my life before Courtney was
even pregnant, though. I've always been fascinated with medical texts and charts. [I] guess I secretly want to be a doctor
or something—I don't know. Or a person that works in a
cremation factory . . . I don't know, I've always liked anatomy,
ever since I was a little kid, when I first got that little model
of The Invisible Man, or The Visible Man. It's just something
I really like.

And since I've become a big rock star and made a bunch
of money, I've found this place in the Mall of America in
Minneapolis that sells nothing but medical stuff. It's a medical supply store that's turned into . . . that they've offered
to the public. It's really great. I bought all these fetuses and,
you know, anatomy men, and charts and stuff, and it is like
a dream come true. 'Cause I've always been really poor, and
if I could find something like that in a secondhand store, I'd
barely have enough money to buy it. A lot of times I *couldn't*
buy that stuff, so I just went on this rampage of buying all

this stuff. And I think I've overused it for, like, pictures for the album and . . . I just went overboard on it.

EHM: You know the old saying, that you can't buy happiness. You think that's true?

COBAIN: [*Laughs*] Well, yeah, you can't buy happiness. I mean, that made me happy for a little while, but I was probably almost as happy with . . . I look back on going to second-hand stores, and stuff like that, and finding a little treasure. And that actually meant more to me because it was more of a stab in the dark, in a way. 'Cause you didn't know if you were going to be able to afford it, and you don't know what you're really looking for. When you find it, it's more special to you, rather than having a thousand dollars and going into a store like that and just buying the whole store, you know? It's not as special.

EHM: Because you've achieved so much success so quickly, so surprisingly, [and] you've had a baby, you've been married—what excites you now?

COBAIN: My baby and my marriage. I don't know. I still like playing, too. I mean, Krist and Dave and I haven't changed at all. Believe it or not, we get along just as well as we ever did. We're just the same passive-aggressive people as we used to be, and we never fight. And when we're pissed off at each other, we just hold it under our breath and have respect for one another in that way. It's easier to work that way because we have a mission, I guess.

EHM: How do you personally cope with having relationships—private relationships—that are always being scrutinized publicly? It must be really difficult.

COBAIN: Well, it is. But I still have a lot of the same friends that I used to have, so . . . They don't seem to mind. And that isn't ever really exposed too much—no one writes about how me and my friend Dillon walked down the street and did whatever. But . . .

EHM: But they rip apart you and Courtney. They love to do that.

COBAIN: Yeah. I don't know why. But we're just . . . I don't know. I guess my ego could be talking right now, and I could say, "Well, we're interesting people." But I think we're just easy scapegoats. It [starts] with something and then people just pick up on it and carry it along, and we turn into cartoon characters. There's nothing I can do about it, really. I can threaten to sue, and bring up libel laws and stuff to people that write shit like that about us. But if you've ever looked into that, it's pretty much a lost cause. You have to have a lot of money to do that. I could spend the money that I earned last year all on fighting the *Vanity Fair* piece, and they'd end up winning, 'cause they have more money.

EHM: There's a magazine in Canada that incorporates itself for each issue. And then it goes bankrupt on each issue, so that it can write whatever it wants, and no one can ever sue them.

COBAIN: Wow, that's a pretty smart thing to do. [*Laughs*]

EHM: Yeah, it is.

COBAIN: That kind of reminds me of how a lot of stations in the States got ahold of our new album, but it was like someone had anonymously sent them fifth-generation cassette copies. And in order for them to play it, they started on the weekend, at five o'clock on Friday nights. That way they could play it throughout the rest of the weekend without having counsel sue them. That's kind of . . . that's kind of smart.

EHM: That's free publicity for you, anyway. Ultimately the album's going to come out.

COBAIN: That's true—but the thing is, there's been so much controversy about how bad the record sounds, you know, and how lo-fi it is. And to hear it like that, compared to all the other songs that were on the radio that night—it really disgusted me and it pissed me off, because it sounded terrible. It sounded really, really bad. Then everyone that heard it that weekend is going to say, "Yeah, you're right. Okay, the stories are true, the Nirvana album really sucks, and I'm not going to buy it." So it just kinda bothered me. But we took care of it.

EHM: What did you do?

COBAIN: Well, I thought maybe we should hire a lawyer to stop them, then instead I just decided to hire a hit man.

EHM: Pardon me? [*Laughs*]

COBAIN: [*Laughs*] Nothing, nothing; erase that. No, we just called them up on Monday and told them to stop.

EHM: And they went, "Oh, okay."

COBAIN: Well, our lawyer did that.

EHM: Is that a weird world for you, to suddenly have lawyers and people who do stuff like that for you?

COBAIN: Yeah. It's totally unnecessary too. If we weren't in this position, we wouldn't need lawyers, you know? It's totally unnecessary, and we have to spend a lot of money just to protect ourselves all the time, and it's just stupid.

EHM: When did that first hit you? When did you realize that you were going to need some people on your team to protect you from the vultures?

COBAIN: Too late. Much after the fact, after we'd already been damaged to a point where it almost doesn't do any good. I don't know, it was just a weird realization one day: "Wow, I have to . . ." I can see how rock and roll stars will all of a sudden—well, almost compromise their music—to make sure that they sell the same amount of records next year, because they've spent all their money on lawyers and protecting themselves *last* year. I mean, we obviously haven't done that. You might not have noticed, but the record isn't as commercial as the last one. We could never bring ourselves to do that. I'd rather just laugh about it.

EHM: I was talking to Aimee Mann, the girl from 'Til Tuesday. She was at her office just a couple of days ago. She's on tour with Ray Davies or the Kinks, and Ray Davies was in the office also, he came in before her. And I had mentioned to her that he was very nice, but really eccentric when I was talking to him—kind of nutty. And she said, "Well, you know, there's a lot of people who have been around the record business for those many years, and most of them are kind of nutty. It just, you know, it makes people nutty." [*Cobain laughs and nods*]

EHM: I mean, you have to—you're facing that, that's your future.

COBAIN: Yeah, that's my future. Hopefully, we'll put out *Metal Machine Music* next year . . . I don't know. Either I've accepted it, or I've gone beyond insane to where I can deal with it, emotionally. I really don't care. I know that I am too stubborn to allow myself to ever compromise our music, or get so wrapped up in it and involved to where it's going to turn us into big rock stars. I just don't feel like that. Everyone else accuses us of it, but we're not as popular as everyone thinks. We're not as rich as everyone thinks. You know? It's just . . . we've always had a good sense of humor; I don't think that's been translated very well. But we'd rather laugh about it. Ha ha ha ha . . .

EHM: What really surprised me, though, is you're . . . you're pretty bright, and your lyrics are, and your whole stage persona is pretty angry, angst-ridden, frustrated. You see the world for what it is. Did you ever have second thoughts about bringing a child into the world, the way it is?

COBAIN: Oh, yeah, absolutely. Yeah. I really can't describe what changed our attitude so fast. I think I really was a lot more negative and angry, and everything else a few years ago, but that had a lot to do with not having a mate, you know, not having a steady girlfriend and stuff like that. That was one of the main things that was bothering me, that I wouldn't admit at the time. So now that I've found that, the world seems a lot better for some reason. It really does change your attitude about things. I mean, four years ago I would have said the classic thing, like "How dare someone bring a child into this life! It's completely a terrible way to go, and the world's gonna explode any day!" and stuff like that. But once you fall in love, it's a bit different.

EHM: I don't want to know about it, stop. [*Laughs*] George [the cameraman] and I are not in the best love situation right now, so stop talking about that. We'll change the subject.

COBAIN: I'm not boasting about it. It's just something that's really weird.

EHM: No, it's nice to hear you talk about it. It's nice. You know, about this whole grunge thing—that's in quotations, "grunge"—all I want to know is, where did the term come from?

COBAIN: I have no idea. I think some of the rumors are that Jonathan Poneman said it one time, sarcastically, and it just caught on

EHM: Who's that?

COBAIN: He's one of the head honchos at Sub Pop Records. But no one set out to market this music as that. That's what happens when the media catches on; they have to call it something. I like it as much as "New Wave." I would have been proud to be a New Waver, you know, fifteen years ago.

EHM: Oh, yeah, we're about the same age. I was into New Wave, absolutely. Do you think you have some of the same . . . is there anything the same between your music and New Wave?

COBAIN: I think so.

EHM: Like what?

COBAIN: Well, like New Wave was just a progression from punk rock, and a mutation of punk rock, and it was more commercial and more palatable. It had punk rock roots, and it was easier to swallow for the media and middle America and the middle of the world. And that's what I kind of think about our music.

EHM: Are you worried about a Nirvana backlash?

COBAIN: Hasn't that already been over with? Hasn't that already happened? I don't know. Sure, I . . . no, I don't know. We're getting more New Wave as the days go by. I think we're going to reinvent New Wave and bring back break dancing. I'd really like to bring back New Wave and break dancing, you know? Meld it to something. That's what our new music is sounding like. We're using a lot more effects boxes and we're . . . We haven't resorted to skinny ties, but we're gonna, our music's . . .

This sounds like the closing of the chapter of the formula we've been using, you know? It's like grunge is really kinda boring for us. It's something we can't deny, and we're not going to stop playing the old songs live . . . But you know, our tastes are changing so rapidly that we're really experimenting with a lot of stuff. And it might get too indulgent and be embarrassing for the next album. But we can't put out another album, and this is just the last chapter of three-chord grunge music for us. And . . . it was an easy thing to do, and a safe thing to do, because we knew it's still popular, you know? But we had to get it out of our systems.

EHM: How come you are so nice and you're . . . you seem so comfortable with yourself. Something must have really happened in the last couple years. Is it just falling in love?

COBAIN: No.

EHM: What happened?

COBAIN: I've always been a nice guy.

EHM: Maybe you were afraid to show it before. How's that?

COBAIN: [*Laughs*] Well, what—I don't know, you've never met me before, so . . .

EHM: I've never met you before. But I know of other people who have had the opportunity to interview you, and they said, "Oh, he hates doing interviews. He's not going to want to talk about anything." I said, "Well, you know, whatever. Who knows?" And you're just, like, exactly the opposite of . . .

COBAIN: It just depends on what mood I'm in, really. I'm kind of a moody person, and a lot of times, when someone has had the chance to talk to me, I've probably been on tour, or I've probably gone through an exhausting time where I've talked about myself for hours and hours. And this week I haven't had to talk about myself very much, so I'm probably more cooperative.

EHM: Lucky me! I think one of the interesting things about Nirvana that you don't really talk about that much, is that you're very concerned about sexism; I like that, that's good. So how do you make people aware of that problem?

COBAIN: By writing songs as blunt as "Rape Me." Having to resort to doing something like that is almost embarrassing, because people didn't understand when we wrote a song like "About a Girl" or "Polly." And having to explain that, and having misunderstandings about it—it's just . . . I decided to write "Rape Me" in a way that was so blunt and obvious that no one could deny it, and no one could read into it any other way.

Although some people *have* actually. Because of some of the lyrics in it, some people have thought that maybe it has something to do with my disgust with the media and the way they've treated us, and stuff like that. But it's not true. That's not what the song's about at all. It's just my way—in a sarcastic way, almost—of saying, "How obvious do we have to be?" I guess we don't talk about those kinds of things that are really important to us, because [we] don't want to be thought of as nothing more than a PC band, you know? We're entertainers, that's what music is. So it's really hard to step over the lines.

EHM: It's that you have so much power because that camera's on you. You can use it.

COBAIN: Yeah. Well, we try to use our power. We really have been effective in certain ways, like being associated with this organization called FAIR [Fairness and Accuracy in Reporting]. And I can't remember right now, 'cause I have a mental block of exactly what it stands for, but it's something like . . . ah, shit, I can't remember. But they're an organization [that] looks at injustices, that looks at the details that surround certain issues and certain stories that have been reported in magazines and newspapers like *USA Today*, who tend to look over a lot of the facts. And they're pretty much a leftist organization that tries to protect people in certain areas, and they supposedly try as hard as they can to deliver the truth.

So we've done benefits like that, "No on 9" benefits to

try to stop Portland's antigay laws that they were trying to pass, and we did a Bosnian benefit and stuff like that. And it doesn't seem like much, but we raised like $50,000 for the Bosnian rape victims, and that's a lot more than we could have done griping about it and talking about it in interviews, and maybe putting out a fanzine . . . You know, there's nothing wrong with doing stuff like that, but we're using the tools that we have and being effective as much as we can. But we still don't want to be too political at the same time, because it's just kind of embarrassing to do that, or you get a lot of ridicule for it.

EHM: Yeah, but you're doing what you believe in, that's the most important thing.

COBAIN: Well, it's hard not to, you know? If you're put in this position, what are you gonna do? Become a Republican or something, just to protect what you've earned? Big deal.

EHM: OK, we're gonna ask a couple more questions, then let you free.

COBAIN: Is it all right to smoke on Canadian television?

EHM: Well, it's too late now, you've already had . . . Sure, do what you want.

COBAIN: I've only had three.

EHM: So, we're doing a special on the Replacements, and I was wondering if they had an influence on you at all as a songwriter, or on the music you make?

COBAIN: I kind of wish they did, because there's so many comparisons to us. I have to be honest: I really didn't like the Replacements when I was into punk rock music. I listened to them, and I liked the sound of it. I don't know if that . . . I think my appreciation for R.E.M., the Beatles, and stuff like that had more to do with it, 'cause I really wasn't aware of Soul Asylum and the Replacements and those bands. I mean, I knew about them, and I actually saw them live and stuff, and I just didn't get it, I didn't like it that much.

EHM: And can we have a comment, please, on . . . I'll wait 'til you light this one, because this is such a . . . What is your comment on Muzak being here . . . of the capital of Muzak being here in Seattle?

COBAIN: Well, it's an obvious thing to happen, you know? Something that you'd expect . . . Oh, oh, I thought you were talking about this Muzak record that they put out, of *Grunge Lite* . . .

EHM: Oh, the *Grunge Lite*, what do you think of that?

COBAIN: It's great, sure. It's an obvious thing to happen. It's the last chapter on the book of grunge. But the Muzak capital? So this is the place where most Muzak comes from? I didn't even know that. I thought there was just one station here.

EHM: Seattle is the capital of Muzak.

COBAIN: Thanks for letting me know about that.

EHM: You thought it was grunge. No! [*Laughs*] Ah, we were there. But they're not doing your songs.

COBAIN: Ah, bummer. [*Laughs*]

EHM: They said it was too aggressive, it would make people too excited.

COBAIN: Oh, well . . . we have some pretty songs, too. God, that's really a bummer. That upsets me. But, I don't know, Muzak, that's pretty neat.

EHM: But they didn't like the *Grunge Lite* album, because the woman sent a copy to them, and they didn't like it because it was too electronic, and they're into using real musicians.

COBAIN: Oh, yeah, I like that idea better too. I liked it when Devo did their Muzak version of their songs, that was really neat. Did you ever hear that? That was nice. And I think they used real musicians for that.

EHM: Did you get to hang out with them, Devo? I know that you're a fan of theirs.

COBAIN: No, never met them.

EHM: Did you get to meet anyone who would be like your hero? Anyone that you're real pleased that you got to meet?

COBAIN: Yeah, yeah, that's kind of a positive side of being a rock and roll star. But actually I met Iggy Pop before we were rock and roll stars, and Iggy Pop is pretty much the only person that I've met that I really, really admire and like.

EHM: And when you met him, were you pleased?

COBAIN: Yeah, it was a big excitement, it was great. I didn't ask him for an autograph. I tried not to bother him the way that I thought that I might be bothered . . . And then the other person is William Burroughs. I met him and I actually got to put out a record with him.

EHM: Tell me about the record that you're doing with William Burroughs.

COBAIN: Well, it's already out, it's just a ten-inch, just one story of his called "The 'Priest' They Called Him," and I just . . . It was a long-distance recording. He had recorded his version and then I just played a bunch of guitar noises in the background, and they mixed it somewhere else. It came out, and now we're talking about putting out a whole album.

EHM: Wow! Of him reading his work and you playing guitar underneath?

COBAIN: I think I'll play a bunch of instruments this time, instead of just fucking off like I did before. It was just a last-minute thing where I just made a bunch of noise, but this time I'd like to work on it—maybe I'll do a Muzak version.

EHM: I'm sure William Burroughs would love that. Let me make sure I have all my questions asked, and this is one that I—oh, Tori Amos—did you like the cover of "Smells Like [Teen Spirit]"?

COBAIN: Well, it served a purpose, because we used that as an opening. Before we came out, we'd play that song, and we would come out and dance to it. Do a little bit of interpretive dancing to it. It was nice.

EHM: The last thing I want to ask you about is . . . I'm not sure who in your band said it—it could have been you, it could have been someone else—but someone being a little perturbed by them, your mainstream audience, and wanting to just make music for your real fans . . .

COBAIN: Well, a couple of years ago when we were making these bold, negative statements about things like that, we were really confused, and we were scared—we were afraid that we would lose a lot of our audience that meant a lot to us, because they're people that we hopefully feel that we have a connection with, you know, the college students and people in the underground. And no, I don't think we've lost them. I think they're still fans. so I'm not worried about it anymore. And I was at the time.

COBAIN ON COBAIN

INTERVIEW BY EDGAR KLÜSENER
AUGUST 10, 1993

EDGAR KLÜSENER: I think the bonus track on the CD, "Gallons of Rubbing Alcohol Flow Through the Strip," it sounds very spontaneous. Did you record that on the spot?

DAVE GROHL: Which song is it? Is it the organ thing?

KURT COBAIN: We made that song up on the spot. I just started playing the guitar part and then Krist and Dave started playing and then, as we were recording, I just made up the lyrics.

KRIST NOVOSELIC: That's the one. We recorded that song in Rio de Janeiro.

GROHL: Oh, yeah.

NOVOSELIC: At this tiny BMG B studio that hasn't been used for, like, six years, they have this Neve board. They blew the dust off it, and we just plugged in and started screwing around. And we did that song; it was totally spontaneous. It was just one of those things.

KLÜSENER: Yeah, it gives that feeling.

NOVOSELIC: It's free association.

KLÜSENER: What the hell does the title mean, anyway?

NOVOSELIC: *In Utero*? I think there's, like, an in vitro pregnancy, then there's conception . . .

KLÜSENER: No, I mean of that song.

NOVOSELIC: Oh, "gallons of rubbing alcohol . . . will cleanse the strip"?

COBAIN: I guess it's our contempt for the hairspray Guns N' Roses/Poison scene that was going on in LA a few years ago.

KLÜSENER: Something else I found out . . . Oh, no, one question beforehand: The way you recorded this was on an 8-track machine, is that true?

GROHL: No, that's not true.

COBAIN: It was a 24-track. It's the same board that recorded *Back in Black* by AC/DC.

KLÜSENER: And what was the story that some of the songs have been remixed?

COBAIN: Two songs were remixed.

KLÜSENER: Which were?

COBAIN: "Heart-Shaped Box" and "All Apologies." 'Cause the vocals weren't loud enough and I wanted to put some harmony vocals in the background that I failed to do when we recorded with Steve [Albini], so we asked [producer] Scott Litt to come down and do it. It took about a day or two.

NOVOSELIC: Yeah. Complete.

KLÜSENER: But I noticed this, not only on this record but on the records before too: there are some very fine harmonies and melodies on it. Which makes me wonder: Does one of you have a sort of musical education?

COBAIN: Absolutely not.

GROHL: I don't think any of us did.

COBAIN: I have no concept of knowing how to be a musician at all, whatsoever. I mean, I don't know the names of chords to play; I don't know how to do major and minor chords on a guitar at all. I couldn't even pass Guitar 101—full Guitar 101, you know? Everyone knows more than I do.

NOVOSELIC: I took accordion lessons when I was a little kid.

GROHL: I played the trombone, I think when I was about eight.

COBAIN: I was in band, and I played snare drum during junior high and grade school. I never learned how to read music.

I just copied the other people who took the time to learn how to read, and it was just so simple, you know? Boom tap boom tap boom tap-tap tap tap . . .

GROHL: He's a good drummer . . .

COBAIN: And I just copied them, you know, just to pass. Even at that age, I didn't see any reason to learn anything that someone else has written. If you go by a text, then your pretty limited.

* * *

KLÜSENER: Do you consider yourself more of a songwriter or a guitar player?

COBAIN: Oh, songwriter. I have no desire to become any better of a guitar player. I just don't. I'm not into musicianship at all. I don't have any respect for it, I just hate it. To learn how to read music or to understand arpeggios and Dorian modes and all that stuff, it's just a waste of time. It gets in the way of originality.

KLÜSENER: Do you like Leonard Cohen?

COBAIN: Mmm-hmm.

KLÜSENER: And are there other artists you could name as sort of an influence, or people who impressed you in what they were doing?

COBAIN: Well, yeah. It's mostly early- to late-eighties punk rock. American punk rock and late-seventies English punk rock had a lot to do with stuff that I was into. I was just pretty much consumed with that whole scene for so long that I never really denied any of the other influences that I had before.

KLÜSENER: What about writers, like lyricists or poets?

COBAIN: Uh, probably Beckett's my favorite. I like him a lot.

KLÜSENER: Sometimes when I read or listen to the lyrics, it sounds to me as if you're sort of inspired by the Beat writers too, especially Burroughs.

COBAIN: Yeah, Burroughs is the king, yeah! I actually got to do a record with him, a ten-inch record.

KLÜSENER: You are doing one?

COBAIN: Its already out, yeah. He did a passage from a poem called "The 'Priest' They Called Him," and I played guitar in the background, just made a bunch of noise.

KLÜSENER: What is this guy like?

COBAIN: Just, um . . . I don't know. I never met him. [*Laughs*] I could have talked to him the other day. I was supposed to . . . there was a meeting set up for him to call me because we wanted him to be in our next video. Not because of our association with him, or to exploit anything like that—because

I don't want anyone to think that I want to have a relationship with William Burroughs because of my past drug use or my respect for him or anything. We mainly wanted him to be in our video because he's an odd-looking character, you know? We wanted an older gentleman to be in our video and to do a few things, but we realized that the things we wanted this older person to do, it was a bit degrading to have William Burroughs himself do it. We wanted a person to be on a cross and in a hospital bed and stuff like that. And it was just too insulting to ask him, so I canceled the call. I mean, that was my chance of actually meeting him. We've exchanged a letter through fax, and we have respect for what each other does, but I've never really had the opportunity . . . I mean, other than that, I haven't bothered to meet him yet. But I still want to.

KLÜSENER: Yeah, he must be a great guy. I would love to meet him one day.

COBAIN: Yeah. His letter was really nice.

KLÜSENER: On one or two songs you hear a cello or some string arrangement. Was that played live?

COBAIN: No, we had her come in after the basic tracks were down, and had her play along with it.

KLÜSENER: Is that the cello player you had in New York too?

COBAIN: No, this cello player was Steve Albini's girlfriend at

the time. It was just a matter of convenience. She happened
to play cello and we needed one, so she was there. She turned
out great, she did a really good job.

KLÜSENER: Another question, for Kurt again: Since you're
left-handed, do you find it hard to get the right guitar?

COBAIN: Usually yeah. It's a bit easier now because I have
an endorsement with Fender guitars. They're making me
left-handed Mustangs, so it's a lot easier. It used to be a total
pain in the ass. When we were on our first couple of tours,
I'd only have one guitar, and it would have to be cheap—
you know, a thirty-dollar guitar from a pawn shop—and I'd
end up breaking it after the show. Then the next day I was
consumed with trying to find a pawn shop and the few dollars we had to buy a guitar. And then we'd have to turn the
strings around and try to intonate it ourselves. It just made
for a really out-of-tune, raunchy experience during those
first few years.

NOVOSELIC: It was a pain in the ass trying to find a guitar.

COBAIN: Yeah, it was like the biggest dilemma of the day.

NOVOSELIC: This one will work left-handed, yeah, it's cut—
this part's notched a little bit . . .

COBAIN: It was a big hassle.

NOVOSELIC: The electronics are in the top.

COBAIN: In fact, we even built a bunch of Mustangs one time. We bought some necks and took pieces of wood and cut out the bodies and put the necks on, and they were completely out of tune all the time—but we did a pretty good job at it.

NOVOSELIC: We had this little assembly line in the garage, and we hung them up and painted them and stuff, yeah. [*Laughs*]

KLÜSENER: You used some quite unique-looking guitars on stage, anyway. Were those the ones you built yourselves?

COBAIN: Um, I don't think so. Those were all destroyed in one tour. That was about four years ago, probably, at least. The ones I use now are just . . . I use this same Jaguar a lot, and mostly Mustangs. And I'm having Fender build me a special guitar that's like a mixture of a Mustang and a Jaguar, which might be kind of interesting

KLÜSENER: Did you give them directions for what you wanted?

COBAIN: Yeah, I took a picture of a Jaguar with a Polaroid, and a picture of a Mustang, and then cut them down the middle and glued them together and said, "Build this."

KLÜSENER: This record, *In Utero*, is getting more back toward *Bleach*. And you said months ago that you want to get rid of some of the fans who came from the pop side. Do you think you will achieve that? Or has the name Nirvana already gone so big that the fans will buy anything, it doesn't matter what it sounds like?

COBAIN: I don't know. I don't think so, because when we put out *Incesticide* it didn't sell very well at all. It didn't even sell a few hundred thousand copies, you know?

NOVOSELIC: We don't want to exclude anybody or anything, you know?

COBAIN: No, we're not as concerned with that as we used to be? It's not . . .

NOVOSELIC: I think it was being a little reactionary, going through the whole fame and fortune thing and making statements like that . . .

COBAIN: There's nothing you can do about it, you know? You can put on a cabaret show and make a total mockery out of your success, or just deal with it.

KLÜSENER: I guess, especially in the beginning, it must have been pretty hard to deal with that.

COBAIN: Yeah, it was. 'Cause we were really concerned with losing the audience that was into us before. We still wanted those people because we feel like we relate to them in a way. I mean, those are the kind of people that we share common interests with, and those are the people that we're friends with. So we were really worried about that. I don't think we've lost very many of them, so it doesn't matter anymore. As long as they're there, we can just forget about the idiots in the back, as long as they aren't causing trouble. That was another concern that we had, is that, if we were to have this massively mainstream audience, we were going to come across a lot of problems in live shows with macho guys beating up on girls, starting fights, and things like that. You know, the typical things that you see at a Van Halen show. We didn't want to have to deal with something like that.

* * *

KLÜSENER: Do you sometimes have the feeling that you lose intensity when you play these big arenas or big places?

COBAIN: I don't find myself having as much fun as I did when we played in clubs or theaters. The biggest example of that is when we played in Europe and played all these outdoor festivals. I had a terrible time. I hated it. Krist and Dave were, like, thirty feet away from me, you know? It was like [*he waves*] "Hi!" It just didn't seem right. So we're gonna make a few changes in our stage setup to alleviate some of those problems. We're gonna squeeze closer together on these big stages. And whether that fucks with the visuals for the people out in the audience . . . oh, well. At least we'll play better and enjoy ourselves.

NOVOSELIC: We played in front of a hundred thousand people down in São Paulo, Brazil, and I saw the video from the back of the stadium. We were just like little ants on stage. Like who's standing there? I wonder how they feel about that.

GROHL: I don't think our music translates in that kind of situation, either, because people can't appreciate the energy that is on stage. Because they're so far away.

COBAIN: It's almost understandable why a lot of lead singers in arena rock bands have this rapport with the audience, where they're going "Hey, how's everybody doing? How are you in the back, people?" And stuff like that—"Are you feeling all right?"

NOVOSELIC: "Are you ready to rock?" [*Grohl laughs*]

COBAIN: Because that's pretty much all you can understand when someone's saying something like that over a PA in front of a hundred thousand people. It's hard for us to adapt to that because we just can't do that, we can't bring ourselves to be that ridiculous.

NOVOSELIC: And doing live shows, you try to experience this thing with the audience, reciprocate this feeling, this energy. I don't know how that translates from three thousand people to a hundred thousand people you know? It's mathematically pretty wild.

COBAIN: We need to get a horn section.

KLÜSENER: Are you thinking of employing a second guitar player again?

COBAIN: Yeah, we've hired Pat Smear, who was in the Germs. He's working out great.

NOVOSELIC: He's got good energy. So I think that he'll add that to the band, live. If one of us is kinda slacking that night, I think we can count on him to keep the energy going.

COBAIN: He's the backup engine.

KLÜSENER: I guess it must make your job easier too?

COBAIN: Yeah, it does. It totally relieves me of a lot of unnecessary things that I have to think about.

KLÜSENER: Looking back, do you sometimes sort of regret the major success of *Nevermind*?

NOVOSELIC: I don't.

COBAIN: No, because for the most part I'm pretty convinced that most people like that record. So, the more the merrier. I mean, the more people who can listen to your music and enjoy it, the better it is.

GROHL: If it was some big marketing scheme, then I think I'd probably feel guilty about that. If it was just a contrived thing.

COBAIN: But it just happened organically, more organically than anything has in a long time.

GROHL: It's flattering.

KLÜSENER: You know, especially in the beginning you sometimes had this feeling that even the record company was completely overwhelmed by it, they didn't expect it.

COBAIN: Yeah, they were.

NOVOSELIC: They shipped, like, forty thousand copies and it sold out in a day or two. Then you couldn't get the record for a week . . .

COBAIN: It's nice to know that you can sell your music on the music alone. At the time that it took off, a lot of radio stations were playing it before we had a video, which is an uncommon thing in this day and age.

GROHL: So it's not our pretty faces that are selling the records, it's our music.

NOVOSELIC: And it's so neat.

COBAIN: It's our skilled musicianship.

NOVOSELIC: I walk into the Fred Meyer department store down in Longview, Washington—this tiny town—and I look, and I go, "Oh, there's Mudhoney, there's Sebadoh, there's Sonic Youth!" I go, "This is really great!" And before . . .

COBAIN: Just a couple of years ago that was impossible.

NOVOSELIC: And the kids down there are exposed to that. I think it's really positive.

KLÜSENER: You obviously helped a lot of other bands too.

NOVOSELIC: What happened to us has kinda opened a lot of doors. I think we were in the right place at the right time for rock and roll, because all those old rock dinosaurs, all those poof-di-doo hairspray bands, were just hanging on and doing the same thing, basically emulating Hanoi Rocks over and over again. And it just stagnated, like the Soviet economy or something, you know what I mean?

COBAIN: It got just as boring as grunge will within a year.

GROHL: We did a photo shoot with someone for a cover of a magazine, and he was telling us a story about how Bon Jovi came in with a flannel shirt on and said, "Make me look like Nirvana." And he said, "Well?"

COBAIN: Wow. That's pretty flattering.

GROHL: [*Laughs*] I know! Bon Jovi wants to look like us! You know something's wrong.

COBAIN: That just proves he's a desperate, untalented piece of shit. [*Novoselic and Grohl laugh*]

KLÜSENER: Do you have an explanation for your own success?

NOVOSELIC: Explanation? It's all in the cards.

GROHL: It's a roll of the dice.

COBAIN: It's a lot of luck. Being in the right place at the right time.

NOVOSELIC: I think this whole . . . The old dinosaurs were just holding on as long as possible, and we had this really strong song. And there were no number-one rock records. Maybe R.E.M. was number one, and Metallica came out and stuff—but change has to happen. Part of the whole human experience is change.

GROHL: I think that . . .

NOVOSELIO: Next, we're probably gonna be old hats soon and there's gonna be this young, happening band going on. And they'll probably be slagging us off for being dinosaurs and we'll be defensive, and we'll be so established . . .

COBAIN: Make me look like this new band! [*Laughs*]

NOVOSELIC: Yeah. We will have totally consolidated our relationships with people at MTV, the music labels, different magazines . . .

GROHL: We'll have apologized to everybody!

NOVOSELIC: We're gonna be Establishment, and hopefully someone will come by and . . . kill us.

COBAIN: Begging to be on the cover of *Rolling Stone*: "Please! I'm sorry!"

NOVOSELIC: No, 'cause we're so in, so established: "Cover of *Rolling Stone*—when do you guys want it?" [*Gestures snorting cocaine*] "Here, here's another line for ya!" [*Cobain and Grohl laugh*] We're just totally, totally terrible. We're doing . . . we're hanging out with Arnold Schwarzenegger, yeah.

GROHL: Bruce Willis at the new club.

COBAIN: "Hey I'm a Republican now, Krist!" "Hey, me too!"

GROHL: "Whaddaya say?"

NOVOSELIC: "Well, it was cool until we had to pay 38 percent or 36 percent in taxes. Jeez, you know, we got the shaft when we lived under Reagan, and now we're getting the shaft under Clinton. I say we vote for Pat Buchanan!"

COBAIN: Rush Limbaugh!

NOVOSELIC: Rush Limbaugh, yeah. Those feminazis, huh?

KLÜSENER: I guess that must be a strength for you anyways, suddenly being involved with real big business, like on the financial side, giving you the tax . . .

COBAIN: I'm happy to fucking suffer for . . . I'll be glad to throw out more of the money that I've made if it's gonna be put in the right places, if its gonna help the economy. Everybody should suffer, you know? Everyone should start wearing sweaters and turning their heaters down. I didn't mind standing in gas lines when I was a little kid during [the Carter administration]. I had to sit in the car and wait in line with my dad, and he would just curse Carter all the time—"What a bastard!" The convenience of America is ruined . . .

NOVOSELIC: They still give Carter a bad time.

COBAIN: Yeah. Everybody has to swallow a little bit of bad medicine to make things better, so fuck it.

NOVOSELIC: They're kicking Clinton around, but it's like: remember Nixon? Iran-Contra, Reagan S&L scandals? No one ever brings that up, it's just really crazy.

KLÜSENER: Do you think you as a band have the chance to move something in people's minds? To make them think, or at least get a message across?

COBAIN: Well, it's not like a real conscious goal of ours, or something that we prepared to do. It just emulates the personalities that we have. We've always been conscious of political things as much as our, you know, mental capacity can hold, and we . . . [*Laughs*]

NOVOSELIC: We've just been aware of things, and it kinda surfaces and comes out, just because. That's what happens. We don't have this angle that we're a political band or anything.

COBAIN: We've always tried really hard not to put out too much of an image of being too politically conscious. It gets in the way of the music, 'cause that is more important.

NOVOSELIC: And I think, too, in this country, that people are so apathetic and they're so unconscious in front of their TV sets, and then somebody like us, who has some awareness—it makes it look like we're really aware. We're not! You know what I mean? This is just things we're concerned about and we just talk about them. Just because we talk about them at home, or we talk about them with friends, and just happen to talk about things in interviews.

KLÜSENER: Have you ever had the experience that groups—like political or social groups—try to use you or the success you have with the name?

COBAIN: No, I wouldn't say they've used us. We've had a few offers from some political organizations like the FAIR organization, who has been working for years to expose a lot of injustices and to try to promote real truths in a lot of things that have happened politically. It's like an underground leftist organization that tries to expose the truths that are totally masked over by *USA Today* and magazines like that—you know, right-wing magazines. A lot of the time the truth and the details of a story are never reported. That's what this organization does. So they came to us, and of course we're going to want to do something to help them out, because . . . I wouldn't say anyone's tried to take advantage of us in that way at all.

NOVOSELIC: FAIR is an acronym for "Fairness and Accuracy in Reporting." I think I've been really conscious of what's been going on in the media, with being part of the media, you know? And then I look at the way the press responds, and it's being all over the president or being all over Waco, Texas, or Amy Fisher. It's really interesting. There's a lot of bozos out there who just—they form public opinion. People don't think for themselves, so they [the media] have a big responsibility and they're just basically exploiting it. And there's this group here that's into truth, reality, you know?

* * *

KLÜSENER: Getting back . . .

NOVOSELIC: Where were we? Rock and roll!

KLÜSENER: After all the experience you've had with media all over the world, do you still believe what you read? Or see on television?

NOVOSELIC: Never.

COBAIN: Never. I never did before, but I don't believe even more now. I know that I don't even have the right—it's the only thing I've learned, I don't have the right to make an

opinion on anything that I read or see on television until I
go to the fucking source myself, personally. My attitude has
changed so much in the last couple of years, mainly because
of the crap that's been written about us. I don't even find
myself having many opinions on bands anymore, or putting
them down, or going out of my way to like, or have any kind
of expression about them at all, because I don't know these
people. Bon Jovi could be one of the nicest people in the
world. His music sucks, but I don't even want to bother with
expressing those kinds of opinions anymore, because I know
that there are people, probably in this town right now, talking about us. "So I heard that Krist Novoselic, you know,
blah blah blah . . ."

NOVOSELIC: "With his dog!"

COBAIN: "With his grandmother's dog! And it has AIDS!"

NOVOSELIC: Which is not true, by the way.

KLÜSENER: Does that sometimes affect your private life too?
I mean, your friends or your family are reading these stories
about you.

NOVOSELIC: Yeah. It's weird to talk with your wife's great-
grandparents, and they bring up something, and you're like,
"Man, that's not true at all!" And you have to explain to them
how people have different agendas, each writer has their own
perspective and maybe that magazine editor has an agenda,
you know what I mean? And you're at their mercy, basically,

so all you can do is be as honest as possible, put on a happy face, and roll with the punches.

KLÜSENER: Frankly, what surprised me, even though I'm working in the media, was that there were certain magazines where I thought, "OK, whatever they print was at least well researched, like *Newsweek* in America, which we get in Germany." I found it quite confusing that even they made up stories.

COBAIN: Oh, yeah.

NOVOSELIC: I was surprised about *Newsweek*. I thought they were of a different caliber.

COBAIN: I'm not surprised at all. No magazine has any ethics at all. There isn't any magazine . . .

NOVOSELIC: Mainstream magazine . . .

COBAIN: Yeah, mainstream magazine, that would ever stop a good story. They want to sell magazines. They're in the entertainment business.

NOVOSELIC: Yeah, that's a point right there.

COBAIN: And they use politics as some kind of fucking fake tool to sell their magazines.

NOVOSELIC: Right, right.

KLÜSENER: But in this case, I thought this was the sort of magazine that had a real reputation to lose.

NOVOSELIC: I think we're gonna have to get Dave in, David Gergen.

COBAIN: There's no one who is challenging these magazines, though. There are no protection laws against false things that are written about celebrities. Libel suits are a complete farce. Basically, a libel suit is just a challenge between two people who have a lot of money. Whoever has the most money will win it. And if you go up against Condé Nast or some major corporation that owns a whole bunch of magazines and owns this one magazine that wrote shit about you, they'll just filibuster for years, and you'll spend hundreds of thousands of dollars in challenging them. And you'll end up losing, so there's really . . . You can't even get to that first stage of filing for a libel suit. It's a waste of time.

NOVOSELIC: It's pretty wild, all the relationships between people—the bands and the labels and between magazines and all that stuff. You have someone like . . . Bill Clinton had a bad time, so he hired David Gergen, who started throwing parties for the press corps and started smoothing people over because he had relationships. And whaddaya know, good news coming out of Washington for Clinton. It's this manufactured perception, it's not real, it's all just a charade, you know? The bottom line is Stoli vodka ads on the back page and Marlboro ads. They just get that money, and everything in between isn't really that important. Television, the same way. So we're gonna start our own magazine. It's gonna be called the *Nirv-racker*.

KLÜSENER: The *Nirv-racker*. It's a good name, anyway.

NOVOSELIC: Full of character assassinations left and right. We're gonna schmooze it up with people. Whoever greases our palm the most is gonna get a full cover story, you know what I mean? Step one: Take the guys out for dinner—"I'll have lobster, thank you." Step two: Get them in the show for free. Step three: "Uh, I've got this niece; I wanna get her a Mustang car." "Done!" You're on the cover of *Nirv-racker*. Unscrupulous magazine . . . go ahead.

KLÜSENER: How seriously do you take all these clichés and standards of the business and the roles people play?

NOVOSELIC: Oh, I just think of, like, the wrestling industry: like WWF, World Whatever Federation Wrestling, where there's Hulk Hogan and Roddy Piper and . . . Imagine all the politics going on in there. "He's gonna win this match but, see, he has to lose this match," and "They're gonna be on this TV show." It's like, wow, all the drama, all the egos, personalities . . . World Federation Wrestling—it's like, get me out of here.

KLÜSENER: Yeah. Getting back to the record: Is it incidental that the opening, the intro of "Rape Me," sounds a bit like some part in *Nevermind*?

NOVOSELIC: What part of *Nevermind*? Come on!

GROHL: "Smells Like Teen Spirit." I read the question!

KLÜSENER: I'm just trying to remember that.

GROHL: Well . . . yes!

NOVOSELIC: What was the hit song off the second Knack record?

COBAIN: It's an obvious inside joke.

NOVOSELIC: If you play the hit song off the second Knack record, it sounds like "My Sharona." If you play it backward, it sounds like "My Sharona."

GROHL: Really? Shit!

NOVOSELIC: So that's what we were doing. I recommend playing *In Utero* backward and that's . . . Ooh, I let it slip! Oh, I shouldn't have said that! There's all kinds of "Kurt is dead" stuff, you know. It's total devil worship of the worst kind—altars, virgins . . .

COBAIN: Now some white trash mothers are gonna sue us after they beat their children for a few years, neglect them, and then they kill themselves and blame it on us!

NOVOSELIC: That's right!

GROHL: And then blow their faces off and they look like . . .

NOVOSELIC: "I gave them a good Christian upbringing . . . what happened?"

COBAIN: "I tanned his ass every day; he should have turned out just fine. If it wasn't for that record . . ." [*Laughter*]

KLÜSENER: Because no kids committed suicide yet, listening to a Nirvana song.

COBAIN: Let's hope!

NOVOSELIC: They're committing *social* suicide.

KLÜSENER: This is so typically American. You never get that in Europe or Germany.

NOVOSELIC: Well, this is . . . I don't know. There's a lot of symptoms out there, like kids killing themselves or people walking into McDonalds and blowing people away.

COBAIN: They're always killing people who don't deserve it, though, you know. If you're gonna kill a bunch of people, why not assassinate someone who deserves it?

NOVOSELIC: They don't, they don't show that as a symptom. They just say that's a problem, "random act of violence." But maybe that's a symptom of what kind of country we live in and people's values, you see what I mean? I say they're all just fucked! I'll answer that question first off by saying that everybody's fucked, if you ask me, and then why don't we take it from there? We're all fucked. All right, well, we've established something, some kind of criteria. Like a base to get onto. Maybe we're all . . .

COBAIN: And how are they fucked?

NOVOSELIC: How are they fucked? Well, I don't wanna think about that, because that just involves effort, you know what I mean?

COBAIN: Because then, if I waste my time thinking about it and we create some kind of dialogue about it for a while, then we'll just come back to the conclusion that everybody's fucked.

NOVOSELIC: Everybody's fucked, you know. So you just have to take up smoking, live a leisurely lifestyle, bomb some third-world countries, walk into McDonalds and shopping malls with automatic weapons readily available . . .

COBAIN: Hey, if life gets too tough, just buy an AK-47 and walk into McDonalds. You'll feel better.

NOVOSELIC: Yeah. 'Cause you hate Mondays. What's your favorite day of the week?

KLÜSENER: Pardon?

NOVOSELIC: What's your favorite day of the week?

KLÜSENER: I guess Wednesday.

NOVOSELIC: Wednesday?

KLÜSENER: Yeah.

NOVOSELIC: 'Cause you're in the middle of the week? Mine's Friday, man! TGIF! Thank God it's Friday.

COBAIN: That's a good move.

NOVOSELIC: Or Sunday, because it's the Sabbath, the day of the Lord. But if you're a Seventh-day Adventist, your Sabbath is on a Saturday—and they don't eat meat, by the way, and they seem like nice people. I don't know how preachy they get, so if I was to subscribe to any kind of Christian dogma, it would maybe be Seventh-day Adventist.

COBAIN: I'd be a Jehovah's Witness.

NOVOSELIC: You'd be a Hobo Witness! Kurt's walking around, peddling *Watchtower*s. Hobo Witness!

COBAIN: I'd be a Moron-man, Mormon!

KLÜSENER: Oh, by the way, who's that Frances Farmer who's gonna have her revenge on Seattle?

COBAIN: What? What about it?

NOVOSELIC: What denomination was she? [*Laughs*] Uh, probably Baptist.

COBAIN: You should read *Dreamland* [*Frances Farmer: Shadowland*, by William Arnold] by this PI [*Seattle Post-Intelligencer*] reporter who wrote this book about her. It's really good. You know her story, don't you? She was an actress, she was kind of a foul-mouthed person . . .

NOVOSELIC: What's the poem she wrote?

COBAIN: She hated the whole Hollywood scene, and she expressed her hatred for them publicly. And she also, when she was like . . . I think when she was fifteen, she entered this essay contest when she was living here in Seattle, entitled "God is Dead" [*sic*],* and a lot of people accused her of being a communist. And then she went to New York and was a part of this acting troupe, and it supposedly had communist ties too. So then there's this big conspiracy amongst a judge— a very well-known, prominent judge here in Seattle—and bunch of other people who had ties with Hollywood, and they basically just set her up and ruined her life. They had some pictures taken of her when she was arrested for drunk driving, and it was a big, huge scandal. She eventually was sent to a mental institution and given a lobotomy and raped every day for years, and just totally abused, and ended up working at a Four Seasons restaurant alone and dying by herself. There's still . . .

---

* Farmer's essay was actually titled "God Dies."

NOVOSELIC: It was Bainbridge Island. That's where she was institutionalized. Right over there. It was this old, broken down infirmary there.

COBAIN: For years, every night there were lines of custodians, friends, and people—part of the staff—who would wait in line to rape her. She went through a lot of shit. And it just disgusts me to know that some of the people who were part of that conspiracy are living here in Seattle in their comfortable, cushy little homes with their families. This is twenty, this is forty years after the fact, and it just makes me want to kill them.

NOVOSELIC: He's a just God, not a fair one. That's what the Christians say. "God! Why was there Auschwitz?" "Well, I'm a just God, not a fair one." "Oh, OK." You know?

KLÜSENER: Yeah.

NOVOSELIC: "Why is there Lon Mabon?" "Ask Saint Paul, he'll tell you all about it. He wrote this book called the Bible." "I'm the little Jew that wrote the Bible."

KLÜSENER: Do you already have a tour set up?

COBAIN: Not for Europe. Just for the States. We're gonna take it one tour at a time. I mean, we definitely want to and plan to go over to Europe and Japan, Australia . . .

NOVOSELIC: It'll probably be early January or something like that, we'll be in Europe.

KLÜSENER: Touring must have changed for you quite a lot, too, suddenly being confronted with this giant machinery. I mean, when you play big venues and you don't have a lot of people and equipment and the real organization required . . .

NOVOSELIC: Yeah, we used to drive around just three guys in a van, with all of our gear.

COBAIN: But, you know, compared to a lot of other bands that are on our scale, we only have a handful of roadies, people, and a tour manager and a helper for him. It's like a lot of bands that are bigger than us, or as big as us, have fifty people on the road with them. It's this big, confusing, stupid thing that happens. We're still really down-to-earth in that area, and we may suffer for it a lot of times because we don't get things done, but . . . oh, well.

NOVOSELIC: We save a lot of money. [*Laughter*]

COBAIN: It's just funner and simpler that way.

KLÜSENER: Kurt: Having a family, did that change your attitude toward music at all?

COBAIN: Not toward the music.

KLÜSENER: But toward life combined with it?

COBAIN: I'd say I'm that much more optimistic [*indicates a small amount*]. I mean, I totally—I like having a family. It's fun. It's great. But I'm still angry about a lot of other things in life, so it doesn't really stop me from being angry in music. It hasn't changed us very much.

KLÜSENER: Do you sometimes write together with your wife?

COBAIN: What?

KLÜSENER: Do you sometimes write together with your wife, or create stuff?

COBAIN: Sometimes. We usually . . . I wouldn't say it's really writing, it's just jamming, playing together.

KLÜSENER: I think Royal Penny Tea . . . ?

COBAIN: "Pennyroyal Tea"? Yeah, well, they're covering that song. It's mostly my song, you know. But, um, we just jammed on it together and they want to record a version of it.

KLÜSENER: OK, I'm gonna finish. Thanks a lot! How many more [interviews] do you have to do today?

COBAIN: I don't know.

SUCCESS DOESN'T SUCK

INTERVIEW BY DAVID FRICKE
ROLLING STONE
JANUARY 27, 1994

DAVID FRICKE: Along with everything else that went wrong onstage tonight, you left without playing "Smells Like Teen Spirit." Why?

KURT COBAIN: That would have been the icing on the cake. [*Smiles grimly*] That would have made everything twice as worse.

I don't even remember the guitar solo on "Teen Spirit." It would take me five minutes to sit in the catering room and learn the solo. But I'm not interested in that kind of stuff. I don't know if that's so lazy that I don't care anymore or what. I still like playing "Teen Spirit," but it's almost an embarrassment to play it.

FRICKE: In what way? Does the enormity of its success still bug you?

COBAIN: Yeah. Everyone has focused on that song so much. The reason it gets a big reaction is people have seen it on MTV a million times. It's been pounded into their brains. But I think there are so many other songs that I've written that are as good, if not better, than that song, like "Drain You." That's definitely as good as "Teen Spirit." I love the lyrics, and

I never get tired of playing it. Maybe if it was as big as "Teen Spirit," I wouldn't like it as much.

But I can barely, especially on a bad night like tonight, get through "Teen Spirit." I literally want to throw my guitar down and walk away. I can't pretend to have a good time playing it.

FRICKE: But you must have had a good time writing it.

COBAIN: We'd been practicing for about three months. We were waiting to sign to DGC, and Dave [Grohl] and I were living in Olympia, and Krist [Novoselic] was living in Tacoma. We were driving up to Tacoma every night for practice, trying to write songs. I was trying to write the ultimate pop song. I was basically trying to rip off the Pixies. I have to admit it. [*Smiles*] When I heard the Pixies for the first time, I connected with that band so heavily I should have been *in* that band—or at least in a Pixies cover band. We used their sense of dynamics, being soft and quiet and then loud and hard.

"Teen Spirit" was such a clichéd riff. It was so close to a Boston riff or "Louie Louie." When I came up with the guitar part, Krist looked at me and said, "That is so ridiculous." I made the band play it for an hour and a half.

FRICKE: Where did the line "Here we are now, entertain us" come from?

COBAIN: That came from something I used to say every time I used to walk into a party to break the ice. A lot of times, when you're standing around with people in a room, it's really boring and uncomfortable. So it was "Well, here we are, entertain us. You invited us here."

FRICKE: How did it feel to watch something you'd written in fun, in homage to one of your favorite bands, become the grunge national anthem, not to mention a defining moment in youth marketing?

COBAIN: Actually, we did have our own thing for a while. For a few years in Seattle, it was the Summer of Love, and it was so great. To be able to just jump out on top of the crowd with my guitar and be held up and pushed to the back of the room, and then brought back with no harm done to me—it was a celebration of something that no one could put their finger on.

But once it got into the mainstream, it was over. I'm just tired of being embarrassed by it. I'm beyond that.

FRICKE: This is the first US tour you've done since the fall of '91, just before *Nevermind* exploded. Why did you stay off the road for so long?

COBAIN: I needed time to collect my thoughts and readjust. It hit me so hard, and I was under the impression that I didn't really need to go on tour, because I was making a whole bunch of money. Millions of dollars. Eight million to ten million records sold—that sounded like a lot of money to me. So I thought I would sit back and enjoy it.

I don't want to use this as an excuse, and it's come up so many times, but my stomach ailment has been one of the biggest barriers that stopped us from touring. I was dealing with it for a long time. But after a person experiences chronic pain for five years, by the time that fifth year ends, you're literally insane. I couldn't cope with anything. I was as schizophrenic as a wet cat that's been beaten.

FRICKE: How much of that physical pain do you think you channeled into your songwriting?

COBAIN: That's a scary question, because obviously if a person is having some kind of turmoil in their lives, it's usually reflected in the music, and sometimes it's pretty beneficial. I think it probably helped. But I would give up everything to have good health. I wanted to do this interview after we'd been on tour for a while, and so far, this has been the most enjoyable tour I've ever had. Honestly.

It has nothing to do with the larger venues or people kissing our asses more. It's just that my stomach isn't bothering me anymore. I'm eating. I ate a huge pizza last night. It was so nice to be able to do that. And it just raises my spirits. But then again, I was always afraid that if I lost the stomach problem, I wouldn't be as creative. Who knows? [*Pauses*] I don't have any new songs right now.

Every album we've done so far, we've always had one to three songs left over from the sessions. And they usually have been pretty good, ones that we really liked, so we always had something to rely on—a hit or something that was above average. So this next record is going to be really interesting, because I have absolutely nothing left. I'm starting from scratch for the first time. I don't know what we're going to do.

FRICKE: One of the songs that you cut from *In Utero* at the last minute was "I Hate Myself and I Want to Die." How literally did you mean it?

COBAIN: As literal as a joke can be. Nothing more than a joke. And that had a bit to do with why we decided to take it off. We knew people wouldn't get it; they'd take it too seriously. It was totally satirical, making fun of ourselves. I'm thought of as this pissy, complaining, freaked-out schizophrenic who wants to kill himself all the time. "He isn't satisfied with anything." And I thought it was a funny title. I wanted it to be the title of the album for a long time. But I knew the majority of the people wouldn't understand it.

FRICKE: Have you ever been that consumed with distress or pain or rage that you actually wanted to kill yourself?

COBAIN: For five years during the time I had my stomach problem, yeah. I wanted to kill myself every day. I came very close many times. I'm sorry to be so blunt about it. It was to the point where I was on tour, lying on the floor, vomiting air because I couldn't hold down water. And then I had to play a show in 20 minutes. I would sing and cough up blood.

This is no way to live a life. I love to play music, but something was not right. So I decided to medicate myself.

FRICKE: Even as satire, though, a song like that can hit a nerve. There are plenty of kids out there who, for whatever reasons, really do feel suicidal.

COBAIN: That pretty much defines our band. It's both those contradictions. It's satirical, and it's serious at the same time.

FRICKE: What kind of mail do you get from your fans these days?

COBAIN: [*Long pause*] I used to read the mail a lot, and I used to be really involved with it. But I've been so busy with this record, the video, the tour, that I haven't even bothered to look at a single letter, and I feel really bad about it. I haven't even been able to come up with enough energy to put out our fanzine, which was one of the things we were going to do to combat all the bad press, just to be able to show a more realistic side of the band.

But it's really hard. I have to admit I've found myself doing the same things that a lot of other rock stars do or are forced to do. Which is not being able to respond to mail, not being able to keep up on current music, and I'm pretty much locked away a lot. The outside world is pretty foreign to me.

I feel very, very lucky to be able to go out to a club. Just the other night, we had a night off in Kansas City, Missouri, and Pat [Smear] and I had no idea where we were or where to go. So we called up the local college radio station and asked them what was going on. And they didn't know! So we happened to call this bar, and the Treepeople from Seattle were playing.

And it turns out I met three really, really nice people there, totally cool kids that were in bands. I really had a good time with them, all night. I invited them back to the hotel. They stayed there. I ordered room service for them. I probably went overboard, trying to be accommodating. But it was really great to know that I can still do that, that I can still find friends.

And I didn't think that would be possible. A few years ago, we were in Detroit, playing at this club, and about ten people showed up. And next door, there was this bar, and Axl Rose came in with ten or fifteen bodyguards. It was this huge extravaganza; all these people were fawning over him. If he'd just walked in by himself, it would have been no big deal. But he wanted that. You create attention to attract attention.

FRICKE: Where do you stand on Pearl Jam now? There were rumors that you and Eddie Vedder were supposed to be on that *Time* magazine cover together.

COBAIN: I don't want to get into that. One of the things I've learned is that slagging off people just doesn't do me any good. It's too bad, because the whole problem with the feud between Pearl Jam and Nirvana had been going on for so long and has come so close to being fixed.

FRICKE: It's never been entirely clear what this feud with Vedder was about.

COBAIN: There never was one. I slagged them off because I didn't like their band. I hadn't met Eddie at the time. It was my fault; I should have been slagging off the record company instead of them. They were marketed—not probably against their will—but without them realizing they were being pushed into the grunge bandwagon.

FRICKE: Don't you feel any empathy with them? They've been under the same intense follow-up-album pressure as you have.

COBAIN: Yeah, I do. Except I'm pretty sure that they didn't go out of their way to challenge their audience as much as we did with this record. They're a safe rock band. They're a pleasant rock band that everyone likes. [*Laughs*] God, I've had much better quotes in my head about this.

It just kind of pisses me off to know that we work really hard to make an entire album's worth of songs that are as good as we can make them. I'm gonna stroke my ego by saying that we're better than a lot of bands out there. What I've realized is that you only need a couple of catchy songs on an album, and the rest can be bullshit Bad Company rip-offs, and it doesn't matter. If I was smart, I would have saved most of the songs off *Nevermind* and spread them out over a fifteen-year period. But I can't do that. All the albums I ever liked were albums that delivered a great song, one after another: Aerosmith's *Rocks*, the Sex Pistols' *Never Mind the Bollocks* . . . , *Led Zeppelin II*, *Back in Black*, by AC/DC.

FRICKE: You've also gone on record as being a big Beatles fan.

COBAIN: Oh, yeah. John Lennon was definitely my favorite Beatle, hands down. I don't know who wrote what parts of what Beatles songs, but Paul McCartney embarrasses me. Lennon was obviously disturbed. [*Laughs*] So I could relate to that.

And from the books I've read—and I'm so skeptical of anything I read, especially in rock books—I just felt really sorry for him. To be locked up in that apartment. Although he was totally in love with Yoko and his child, his life was a prison. He was imprisoned. It's not fair. That's the crux of the problem that I've had with becoming a celebrity—the way people deal with celebrities. It needs to be changed; it really does.

No matter how hard you try, it only comes out like you're bitching about it. I can understand how a person can feel that way and almost become obsessed with it. But it's so hard to convince people to mellow out. Just take it easy, have a little bit of respect. We all shit. [*Laughs*]

FRICKE: *In Utero* may be the most anticipated, talked-about and argued-over album of 1993. Didn't you feel at any point during all the title changes and the press hoopla stirred up by Steve Albini that the whole thing was just getting stupid? After all, it is just an album.

COBAIN: Yeah. But I'm used to it. [*Laughs*] While making the record, that wasn't happening. It was made really fast. All the basic tracks were done within a week. And I did 80 percent of the vocals in one day, in about seven hours. I just happened to be on a roll. It was a good day for me, and I just kept going.

FRICKE: So what was the problem?

COBAIN: It wasn't the songs. It was the production. It took a very, very long time for us to realize what the problem was. We couldn't figure it out. We had no idea why we didn't feel the same energy that we did from *Nevermind*. We finally came to the conclusion that the vocals weren't loud enough, and the bass was totally inaudible. We couldn't hear any notes that Krist was playing at all.

I think there are a few songs on *In Utero* that could have been cleaned up a little bit more. Definitely "Pennyroyal Tea." That was not recorded right. There is something wrong with that. That should have been recorded like *Nevermind*, because I know that's a strong song, a hit single. We're toying with the idea of re-recording it or remixing it.

You hit and miss. It's a really weird thing about this record. I've never been more confused in my life, but at the same time I've never been more satisfied with what we've done.

FRICKE: Let's talk about your songwriting. Your best songs— "Teen Spirit," "Come As You Are," "Rape Me," "Pennyroyal Tea"—all open with the verse in a low, moody style. Then the chorus comes in at full volume and nails you. So which comes first, the verse or the killer chorus?

COBAIN: [*Long pause, then he smiles*] I don't know. I really don't know. I guess I start with the verse and then go into the chorus. But I'm getting so tired of that formula. And it is formula. And there's not much you can do with it. We've mastered that—for our band. We're all growing pretty tired of it.

It is a dynamic style. But I'm only using two of the dynamics. There are a lot more I could be using. Krist, Dave and I have been working on this formula—this thing of going from quiet to loud—for so long that it's literally becoming boring for us. It's like "OK, I have this riff. I'll play it quiet, without a distortion box, while I'm singing the verse.

And now let's turn on the distortion box and hit the drums harder."

I want to learn to go in between those things, go back and forth, almost become psychedelic in a way but with a lot more structure. It's a really hard thing to do, and I don't know if we're capable of it—as musicians.

FRICKE: Songs like "Dumb" and "All Apologies" do suggest that you're looking for a way to get to people without resorting to the big-bang guitar effect.

COBAIN: Absolutely. I wish we could have written a few more songs like those on all the other albums. Even to put "About a Girl" on *Bleach* was a risk. I was heavily into pop, I really liked R.E.M., and I was into all kinds of old '60s stuff. But there was a lot of pressure within that social scene, the underground—like the kind of thing you get in high school. And to put a jangly R.E.M. type of pop song on a grunge record, in that scene, was risky.

We have failed in showing the lighter, more dynamic side of our band. The big guitar sound is what the kids want to hear. We like playing that stuff, but I don't know how much longer I can scream at the top of my lungs every night, for an entire year on tour. Sometimes I wish I had taken the Bob Dylan route and sang songs where my voice would not go out on me every night, so I could have a career if I wanted.

FRICKE: So what does this mean for the future of Nirvana?

COBAIN: It's impossible for me to look into the future and say

I'm going to be able to play Nirvana songs in 10 years. There's no way. I don't want to have to resort to doing the Eric Clapton thing. Not to put him down whatsoever; I have immense respect for him. But I don't want to have to change the songs to fit my age. [*Laughs*]

FRICKE: The song on *In Utero* that has whipped up the most controversy is "Rape Me." It's got a brilliant hook, but there have been objections to the title and lyric—not just from skittish DJs but from some women who feel it's rather cavalier for a man to be using such a potent, inflammatory word so freely.

COBAIN: I understand that point of view, and I've heard it a lot. I've gone back and forth between regretting it and trying to defend myself. Basically, I was trying to write a song that supported women and dealt with the issue of rape. Over the last few years, people have had such a hard time understanding what our message is, what we're trying to convey, that I just decided to be as bold as possible. How hard should I stamp this point? How big should I make the letters?

It's not a pretty image. But a woman who is being raped, who is infuriated with the situation . . . it's like "Go ahead, rape me, just go for it, because you're gonna get it." I'm a firm believer in karma, and that motherfucker is going to get what he deserves, eventually. That man will be caught, he'll go to jail, and *he'll* be raped. "So rape me, do it, get it over with. Because you're gonna get it worse."

FRICKE: What did your wife, Courtney, think of the song when she heard it?

COBAIN: I think she understood. I probably explained it better to her than I've explained it to you. I also want to make a point that I was really, honestly not trying to be controversial with it. That was the last thing I wanted to do. We didn't want to put it out so it would piss off the parents and get some feminists on our asses, stuff like that. I just have so much contempt for someone who would do something like that [to a woman]. This is my way of saying: "Do it once, and you may get away with it. Do it a hundred times. But you're gonna get it in the end."

FRICKE: When you were arrested on the domestic violence charge this summer, Courtney admitted to the police that you kept guns in your home. Why do you feel you need to be armed?

COBAIN: I like guns. I just enjoy shooting them.

FRICKE: Where? At what?

COBAIN: [*Laughs*] When we go out to the woods, at a shooting range. It's not an official shooting range, but it's allowed to be one in this county. There's a really big cliff, so there's no chance of shooting over the cliff and hurting anyone. And there's no one within miles around.

FRICKE: Without getting too PC about it, don't you feel it's dangerous to keep them in the house, especially with your daughter, Frances, around?

COBAIN: No. It's protection. I don't have bodyguards. There are people way less famous than I am or Courtney who have been stalked and murdered. It could be someone by chance looking for a house to break into. We have a security system. I actually have one gun that is loaded, but I keep it safe, in a cabinet high up on a shelf where Frances can never get to it.

And I have an M16, which is fun to shoot. It's the only sport I have ever liked. It's not something I'm obsessed with or even condone. I don't really think much of it.

FRICKE: How does Courtney feel about keeping guns at home?

COBAIN: She was there when I bought them. Look, I'm not a very physical person. I wouldn't be able to stop an intruder who had a gun or a knife. But I'm not going to stand by and watch my family stabbed to death or raped in front of me. I wouldn't think twice of blowing someone's head off if they did that. It's for protection reasons. And sometimes it's fun to go out and shoot. [*Pauses*] At targets. I want to make that clear. [*Laughs*]

FRICKE: People usually assume that someone who has sold a few million records is really livin' large. How rich are you? How rich do you feel? According to one story, you wanted to buy a new house and put a home studio in it, but your accountant said you couldn't afford it.

COBAIN: Yeah, I can't. I just got a check a while ago for some royalties for *Nevermind*, which is pretty good size. It's weird, though, really weird. When we were selling a lot of records during *Nevermind*, I thought, "God, I'm gonna have like $10 million, $15 million." That's not the case. We do not live large. I still eat Kraft macaroni and cheese—because I like it, I'm used to it. We're not extravagant people.

I don't blame any kid for thinking that a person who sells ten million records is a millionaire and set for the rest of his life. But it's not the case. I spent a million dollars last year, and I have no idea how I did it. Really. I bought a house for $400,000. Taxes were another $300,000—something. What else? I lent my mom some money. I bought a car. That was about it.

FRICKE: You don't have much to show for that million.

COBAIN: It's surprising. One of the biggest reasons we didn't go on tour when *Nevermind* was really big in the States was because I thought: "Fuck this, why should I go on tour? I have this chronic stomach pain, I may die on this tour, I'm selling a lot of records, I can live the rest of my life off a million dollars." But there's no point in even trying to explain that to a fifteen-year-old kid. I never would have believed it.

FRICKE: Do you worry about the impact that your work, lifestyle and ongoing war with supercelebrity are having on Frances? She seemed perfectly content to toddle around in the dressing room tonight, but it's got to be a strange world for her.

COBAIN: I'm pretty concerned about it. She seems to be attracted to almost anyone. She loves anyone. And it saddens

me to know that she's moved around so much. We do have
two nannies, one full-time and another older woman who
takes care of her on weekends. But when we take her on the
road, she's around people all the time, and she doesn't get to
go to the park very often. We try as hard as we can, we take
her to preschool things. But this is a totally different world.

FRICKE: In "Serve the Servants," you sing, "I tried hard to
have a father/But instead I had a dad." Are you concerned
about making the same mistakes as a father that might have
been made when you were growing up?

COBAIN: No. I'm not worried about that at all. My father and
I are completely different people. I know that I'm capable
of showing a lot more affection than my dad was. Even if
Courtney and I were to get divorced, I would never allow us
to be in a situation where there are bad vibes between us in
front of [Frances]. That kind of stuff can screw up a kid, but
the reason those things happen is because the parents are not
very bright.

  I don't think Courtney and I are that fucked up. We
have lacked love all our lives, and we need it so much that if
there's any goal that we have, it's to give Frances as much love
as we can, as much support as we can. That's the one thing
that I know is not going to turn out bad.

FRICKE: What has been the state of relations within Nirvana
over the past year?

COBAIN: When I was doing drugs, it was pretty bad. There was no communication. Krist and Dave, they didn't understand the drug problem. They'd never been around drugs. They thought of heroin in the same way that I thought of heroin before I started doing it. It was just really sad. We didn't speak very often. They were thinking the worst, like most people would, and I don't blame them for that. But nothing is ever as bad as it seems. Since I've been clean, it's gone back to pretty much normal.

Except for Dave. I'm still kind of concerned about him, because he still feels like he can be replaced at any time. He still feels like he . . .

FRICKE: Hasn't passed the audition?

COBAIN: Yeah. I don't understand it. I try to give him as many compliments as I can. I'm not a person who gives compliments very often, especially at practice. "Let's do this song, let's do that song, let's do it over." That's it. I guess Dave is a person who needs reassurance sometimes. I notice that, so I try and do that more often.

FRICKE: So you call all the shots?

COBAIN: Yeah. I ask their opinions about things. But ultimately, it's my decision. I always feel weird saying that; it feels egotistical. But we've never argued. Dave, Krist and I have never screamed at each other. Ever.

It's not like they're afraid to bring up anything. I always ask their opinion, and we talk about it. And eventually, we all come to the same conclusions.

FRICKE: Haven't there been any issues where there was at least heated discussion?

COBAIN: Yeah, the songwriting royalties. I get all the lyrics. The music, I get 75 percent, and they get the rest. I think that's fair. But at the time, I was on drugs when that came up. And so they thought that I might start asking for more things. They were afraid that I was going to go out of my mind and start putting them on salary, stuff like that. But even then we didn't yell at each other. And we split everything else evenly.

FRICKE: With all of your reservations about playing "Smells Like Teen Spirit" and writing the same kind of song over and over, do you envision a time when there is no Nirvana? That you'll try to make it alone?

COBAIN: I don't think I could ever do a solo thing, the Kurt Cobain Project.

FRICKE: Doesn't have a very good ring to it, either.

COBAIN: No. [*Laughs*] But yes, I would like to work with people who are totally, completely the opposite of what I'm doing now. Something way out there, man.

FRICKE: That doesn't bode well for the future of Nirvana and the kind of music you make together.

COBAIN: That's what I've been kind of hinting at in this whole interview. That we're almost exhausted. We've gone to the point where things are becoming repetitious. There's not something you can move up toward, there's not something you can look forward to.

The best times that we ever had were right when *Nevermind* was coming out and we went on that American tour where we were playing clubs. They were totally sold out, and the record was breaking big, and there was this massive feeling in the air, this vibe of energy. Something really special was happening.

I hate to actually even say it, but I can't see this band lasting more than a couple more albums, unless we really work hard on experimenting. I mean, let's face it. When the same people are together doing the same job, they're limited. I'm really interested in studying different things, and I know Krist and Dave are as well. But I don't know if we are capable of doing it together. I don't want to put out another record that sounds like the last three records.

I know we're gonna put out one more record, at least, and I have a pretty good idea what it's going to sound like: pretty ethereal, acoustic, like R.E.M.'s last album. If I could write just a couple of songs as good as what they've written . . . I don't know how that band does what they do. God, they're the greatest. They've dealt with their success like saints, and they keep delivering great music.

That's what I'd really like to see this band do. Because we are stuck in such a rut. We have been labeled. R.E.M. is what? College rock? That doesn't really stick. Grunge is as potent a term as New Wave. You can't get out of it. It's going to be passé. You have to take a chance and hope that either a totally different audience accepts you or the same audience grows with you.

FRICKE: And what if the kids just say, "We don't dig it, get lost"?

COBAIN: Oh, well. [*Laughs*] Fuck 'em.

THE LAST INTERVIEW

INTERVIEW BY CHUCK CRISAFULLI
FENDER FRONTLINE MAGAZINE
FEBRUARY 11, 1994

CHUCK CRISAFULLI: Nirvana has become a "Big Rock Story," but the music still seems to be the most important part of that story. Your music offers the simple, powerful rock and roll thrill that so many other bands seem to have a hard time delivering. How proud are you of Nirvana's work?

KURT COBAIN: It's interesting because, while there's a certain gratification in having any number of people buy your records and come to see you play, none of that holds a candle to simply hearing a song that I've written played by a band. I'm not talking about radio or MTV. I just really like playing these songs with a good drummer and bass player. Next to my wife and daughter, there's nothing that brings me more pleasure.

I'm extremely proud of what we've accomplished together. Having said that, however, I don't know how long we can continue as Nirvana without a radical shift in direction. I have lots of ideas and musical ambitions that have nothing to do with this mass conception of "grunge" that has been force-fed to the record-buying public for the past few years. Whether I will be able to do everything I want to do as part of Nirvana remains to be seen. To be fair, I also know that both Krist and Dave have musical ideas that may not work within the context of Nirvana. We're all tired of being labeled. You can't imagine how stifling it is.

CRISAFULLI: You've made it clear that you're not particularly comfortable being a "Rock Star," but one of the things that tracks like "Heart-Shaped Box" and "Pennyroyal Tea" on *In Utero* make clear is that you're certainly a gifted songwriter. You may have a tough time sometimes, but has the written process continued to be pleasurable and satisfying for you?

COBAIN: I think that it becomes less pleasurable when I think of it in terms of being my "job." Writing is the one part that is not a job, it's expression. Photo shoots, interviews . . . that's the real job part.

CRISAFULLI: You're a very passionate performer. Do you find yourself re-experiencing the tenderness and rage in your songs when you perform them?

COBAIN: That's tough, because the real core of any tenderness or rage is tapped the very second that a song is written. In a sense, I'm only recreating the purity of that particular emotion every time I play that particular song. While it gets easier to summon those emotions with experience, it's sort of dishonesty in that you can never recapture the emotion of a song completely each time you play it. Real "performing" implies a sort of acting that I've always tried to avoid.

CRISAFULLI: It must be a very odd feeling for Nirvana to be performing in sports arenas these days. How do you get along with the crowds you're attracting now?

COBAIN: Much better than I used to. When we first got successful, I was extremely judgmental of the people in the audience. I held them up to a sort of punk-rock ethos. It used to upset me that we were attracting and entertaining the very people that a lot of my music was a reaction against. I've since become much better about accepting people for who they are. Regardless of who they are before they came to the show, I get a few hours to try and subvert the way they view the world. It's not that I'm trying to dictate, it's just that I'm afforded a certain platform on which I can express my views. At the very least, I always get the last word.

CRISAFULLI: There's also a great deal of craft in your songs, but you also seem to enjoy the thrill of simply cranking up an electric guitar. Is playing guitar a pleasure for you, or do you battle with the instrument?

COBAIN: The battle is the pleasure. I'm the anti–guitar hero— I can barely play the thing myself. I'm the first to admit that I'm no virtuoso. I can't play like Segovia. The flip side of that is that Segovia could probably never have played like me.

CRISAFULLI: With Pat Smear playing guitar in the touring lineup, has your approach to the instrument changed much? Is it easier to enjoy playing live with an extra pair of guitar hands helping you out?

COBAIN: Pat has worked out great from day one. In addition to being one of my closest friends, Pat has found a niche in our music that complements what was already there, without forcing any major changes. While I don't see myself ever becoming Mick Jagger, having Pat on stage has freed me to spend more time concentrating on my connection with the audience. I've become more of a showman—well maybe that's going a little too far. Let's just say that having Pat to hold down the rhythm allows me to concentrate on the performance as a whole. I think it's improved our live show 100 percent.

CRISAFULLI: On *In Utero*, and in concert, you play some of the most powerful "anti-solos" ever hacked out of a guitar. What comes to mind for you when it's time for the guitar to cut loose?

COBAIN: Less than you could ever imagine.

CRISAFULLI: Krist and Dave do a great job of helping to bring your songs to life. How do you describe the role of each player, including yourself, in the Nirvana sound?

COBAIN: While I can do a lot of switching the channels on my amp, it's Dave who really brings the physicality to the dynamics in our songs. Krist is great at keeping everything going along on some kind of even keel. I'm just the folk singer in the middle.

CRISAFULLI: Aside from interviews, what are the biggest drags for you these days?

COBAIN: Being apart from my family for months at a time. Having people feed me fine French meals when all I want is macaroni and cheese. Being seen as unapproachable when I used to be called shy. Did I mention interviews?

CRISAFULLI: *Nevermind* changed your life in a big way, but having Courtney and Frances around must help you to keep things in perspective. How much do you enjoy being a family man?

COBAIN: It's more important than anything else in the whole world. Playing music is what I do; my family is what I am. When everyone's forgotten about Nirvana and I'm on some revival tour opening for the Temptations and the Four Tops, Frances Bean will still be my daughter and Courtney will still be my wife. That means more than anything else to me.

KURT COBAIN was born on February 20, 1967 in Aberdeen, Washington. He founded his band Nirvana in 1988 with Chad Channing (drums) and Kris Novoselic (bass); Channing was replaced by Dave Grohl in 1990. The band's second album, *Nevermind*, was released on September 24, 1991; an instant classic, it vaulted Cobain and his band into the stratosphere of pop stardom. With his snarling singing, buzzsaw guitar playing, and unexpectedly poetic lyrics, Cobain set the template for what would become known as "grunge" music and became the ultimate Generation X icon. Cobain married Hole singer and guitarist Courtney Love in February 1992, with the birth of the couple's daughter, Frances Bean Cobain, following in August. He died on April 5, 1994. Cobain and Nirvana were inducted into the Rock and Roll Hall of Fame in April 2014, their first year of eligibility.

CHUCK CRISAFULLI'S writing has appeared in *Rolling Stone*, *Billboard*, and *Interview*. He records and performs under the name Charlie Christmas.

ERICA EHM is a writer, podcaster, and media consultant based in Ontario, Canada. She has received multiple awards for her journalism and content creation.

DAVID FRICKE is senior editor at *Rolling Stone* and host of the podcast *The Writers' Block* on Sirius XM Radio.

EDGAR KLÜSENER, PHD, is a lecturer in history and music at the Bimm Institute in Manchester, UK. He is the author of

Representing Iran in East Germany: Ideology and the media in the German Democratic Republic (2020).

JON SAVAGE writes on music and culture for *The Guardian*. He is the author of *England's Dreaming: Anarchy, Sex Pistols, Punk Rock, and Beyond.*

DANA SPIOTTA is the author of five novels: *Wayward* (forthcoming in July 2021), *Innocents and Others* (2016), winner of the St. Francis College Literary Prize and a finalist for the *Los Angeles Times* Book Prize; *Stone Arabia* (2011), which was a finalist for the National Book Critics Circle Award; *Eat the Document* (2006), which was a finalist for the National Book Award and the winner of the American Academy's Rosenthal Foundation Award; and *Lightning Field* (2001), a New York Times Notable Book. Other awards include a Guggenheim Fellowship, a New York Foundation for the Arts Fellowship, the Rome Prize in Literature, the Premio Pivano, a Creative Capital Award, and the John Updike Prize from the American Academy of Arts and Letters.

THE LAST INTERVIEW SERIES

DIEGO MARADONA: THE LAST INTERVIEW AND OTHER CONVERSATIONS

"Football is the most beautiful sport in the world. If somebody makes a mistake, football need not pay for it. I made a mistake and I paid for it. But the ball does not stain."

$17.99 / $23.99 CAN
978-1-61219-973-3
ebook: 978-1-61219-974-0

JOAN DIDION: THE LAST INTERVIEW AND OTHER CONVERSATIONS

"I'm really tired of this angst business. It seems to me I'm as lively and cheerful as the next person. I laugh, I smile... but I write down what I see."

$17.99 / $23.99 CAN
978-1-68589-011-7
ebook: 978-1-68589-012-4

JANET MALCOLM: THE LAST INTERVIEW AND OTHER CONVERSATIONS

"I did not set out to write about betrayal, but by writing about journalism, and photography I kept bumping into it."

$17.99 / $23.99 CAN
978-1-61219-968-9
ebook: 978-1-68589-012-4

THE LAST INTERVIEW SERIES

JOHN LEWIS: THE LAST INTERVIEW AND OTHER CONVERSATIONS

"Get in good trouble, necessary trouble, and help redeem the soul of America."

$16.99 / $22.99 CAN
978-1-61219-962-7
ebook: 978-1-61219-963-4

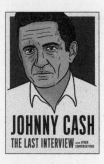

JOHNNY CASH: THE LAST INTERVIEW AND OTHER CONVERSATIONS

"I wouldn't let anybody influence me into thinking I was doing the wrong thing by singing about death, hell, and drugs. Cause I've always done that, and I always will."

$16.99 / $22.99 CAN
978-1-61219-893-4
ebook: 978-1-61219-894-1

FRED ROGERS: THE LAST INTERVIEW AND OTHER CONVERSATIONS

"I think one of the greatest gifts you can give anybody is the gift of your honest self."

$16.99 / $22.99 CAN
978-1-61219-895-8
ebook: 978-1-61219-896-5

THE LAST INTERVIEW SERIES

SHIRLEY CHISHOLM: THE LAST INTERVIEW AND OTHER CONVERSATIONS

"All I can say is that I'm a shaker-upper.
That's exactly what I am.

$16.99 / $22.99 CAN
978-1-61219-897-2
ebook: 978-1-61219-898-9

RUTH BADER GINSBURG : THE LAST INTERVIEW AND OTHER CONVERSATIONS

"No one ever expected me to go to law
school. I was supposed to be a high school
teacher, or how else could I earn a living?"

$17.99 / $23.99 CAN
978-1-61219-919-1
ebook: 978-1-61219-920-7

MARILYN MONROE: THE LAST INTERVIEW AND OTHER CONVERSATIONS

"I'm so many people. They shock me
sometimes.
I wish I was just me!"

$16.99 / $22.99 CAN
978-1-61219-877-4
ebook: 978-1-61219-878-1

THE LAST INTERVIEW SERIES

FRIDA KAHLO: THE LAST INTERVIEW AND OTHER CONVERSATIONS

"The only thing I know is that I paint because I need to, and I paint always whatever passes through my head, without any other consideration."

$16.99 / $22.99 CAN
978-1-61219-875-0
ebook: 978-1-61219-876-7

TONI MORRISON: THE LAST INTERVIEW AND OTHER CONVERSATIONS

"Knowledge is what's important, you know? Not the erasure, but the confrontation of it."

$16.99 / 22.99 CAN
978-1-61219-873-6
ebook: 978-1-61219-874-3

GRAHAM GREENE: THE LAST INTERVIEW AND OTHER CONVERSATIONS

"I think to exclude politics from a novel is to exclude a whole aspect of life."

$16.99 / 22.99 CAN
978-1-61219-814-9
ebook: 978-1-61219-815-6

THE LAST INTERVIEW SERIES

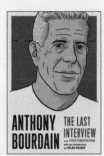

ANTHONY BOURDAIN: THE LAST INTERVIEW AND OTHER CONVERSATIONS

"We should feed our enemies Chicken McNuggets."

$17.99 / $23.99 CAN
978-1-61219-824-8
ebook: 978-1-61219-825-5

URSULA K. LE GUIN: THE LAST INTERVIEW AND OTHER CONVERSATIONS

"Resistance and change often begin in art. Very often in our art, the art of words."

$16.99 / $21.99 CAN
978-1-61219-779-1
ebook: 978-1-61219-780-7

PRINCE: THE LAST INTERVIEW AND OTHER CONVERSATIONS

"That's what you want. Transcendence. When that happens—oh, boy."

$16.99 / $22.99 CAN
978-1-61219-745-6
ebook: 978-1-61219-746-3

THE LAST INTERVIEW SERIES

JULIA CHILD: THE LAST INTERVIEW AND OTHER CONVERSATIONS

"I'm not a chef, I'm a teacher and a cook."

$16.99 / $22.99 CAN
978-1-61219-733-3
ebook: 978-1-61219-734-0

KURT VONNEGUT: THE LAST INTERVIEW

"I think it can be tremendously refreshing if a creator of literature has something on his mind other than the history of literature so far. Literature should not disappear up its own asshole, so to speak."

$15.95 / $17.95 CAN
978-1-61219-090-7
ebook: 978-1-61219-091-4

JACQUES DERRIDA: THE LAST INTERVIEW LEARNING TO LIVE FINALLY

"I am at war with myself, it's true, you couldn't possibly know to what extent... I say contradictory things that are, we might say, in real tension; they are what construct me, make me live, and will make me die."

translated by PASCAL-ANNE BRAULT and MICHAEL NAAS

$15.95 / $17.95 CAN
978-1-61219-094-5
ebook: 978-1-61219-032-7

THE LAST INTERVIEW SERIES

ROBERTO BOLAÑO: THE LAST INTERVIEW

"Posthumous: It sounds like the name of a Roman gladiator, an unconquered gladiator. At least that's what poor Posthumous would like to believe. It gives him courage."

translated by SYBIL PEREZ and others
$15.95 / $17.95 CAN
978-1-61219-095-2
ebook: 978-1-61219-033-4

JORGE LUIS BORGES: THE LAST INTERVIEW

"Believe me: the benefits of blindness have been greatly exaggerated. If I could see, I would never leave the house, I'd stay indoors reading the many books that surround me."

translated by KIT MAUDE
$15.95 / $15.95 CAN
978-1-61219-204-8
ebook: 978-1-61219-205-5

HANNAH ARENDT: THE LAST INTERVIEW

"There are no dangerous thoughts for the simple reason that thinking itself is such a dangerous enterprise."

$15.95 / $15.95 CAN
978-1-61219-311-3
ebook: 978-1-61219-312-0

THE LAST INTERVIEW SERIES

RAY BRADBURY: THE LAST INTERVIEW

"You don't have to destroy books to destroy a culture. Just get people to stop reading them."

$15.95 / $15.95 CAN
978-1-61219-421-9
ebook: 978-1-61219-422-6

JAMES BALDWIN: THE LAST INTERVIEW

"You don't realize that you're intelligent until it gets you into trouble."

$16.99 / $22.99 CAN
978-1-61219-400-4
ebook: 978-1-61219-401-1

GABRIEL GÁRCIA MÁRQUEZ: THE LAST INTERVIEW

"The only thing the Nobel Prize is good for is not having to wait in line."

$15.95 / $15.95 CAN
978-1-61219-480-6
ebook: 978-1-61219-481-3

THE LAST INTERVIEW SERIES

LOU REED: THE LAST INTERVIEW

"Hubert Selby. William Burroughs. Allen Ginsberg. Delmore Schwartz... I thought if you could do what those writers did and put it to drums and guitar, you'd have the greatest thing on earth."

$15.95 / $15.95 CAN
978-1-61219-478-3
ebook: 978-1-61219-479-0

ERNEST HEMINGWAY: THE LAST INTERVIEW

"The most essential gift for a good writer is a built-in, shockproof shit detector."

$15.95 / $20.95 CAN
978-1-61219-522-3
ebook: 978-1-61219-523-0

PHILIP K. DICK: THE LAST INTERVIEW

"The basic thing is, how frightened are you of chaos? And how happy are you with order?"

$15.95 / $20.95 CAN
978-1-61219-526-1
ebook: 978-1-61219-527-8

THE LAST INTERVIEW SERIES

NORA EPHRON: THE LAST INTERVIEW

"You better *make* them care about what you think. It had better be quirky or perverse or thoughtful enough so that you hit some chord in them. Otherwise, it doesn't work."

$15.95 / $20.95 CAN
978-1-61219-524-7
ebook: 978-1-61219-525-4

JANE JACOBS: THE LAST INTERVIEW

"I would like it to be understood that all our human economic achievements have been done by ordinary people, not by exceptionally educated people, or by elites, or by supernatural forces."

$15.95 / $20.95 CAN
978-1-61219-534-6
ebook: 978-1-61219-535-3

DAVID BOWIE: THE LAST INTERVIEW

"I have no time for glamour. It seems a ridiculous thing to strive for... A clean pair of shoes should serve quite well."

$16.99 / $22.99 CAN
978-1-61219-575-9
ebook: 978-1-61219-576-6

HUNTER S. THOMPSON: THE LAST INTERVIEW

"I feel in the mood to write a long weird story—a tale so strange and terrible that it will change the brain of the normal reader forever."

$15.99 / $20.99 CAN
978-1-61219-693-0
ebook: 978-1-61219-694-7

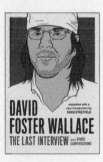

DAVID FOSTER WALLACE: THE LAST INTERVIEW AND OTHER CONVERSATIONS

"I'm a typical American. Half of me is dying to give myself away, and the other half is continually rebelling."

$16.99 / 21.99 CAN
978-1-61219-741-8
ebook: 978-1-61219-742-5

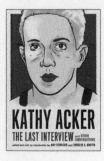

KATHY ACKER: THE LAST INTERVIEW AND OTHER CONVERSATIONS

"To my mind I was in a little cage in the zoo that instead of 'monkey' said 'female American radical.'"

$16.99 / $21.99 CAN
978-1-61219-731-9
ebook: 978-1-61219-732-6

THE LAST INTERVIEW SERIES

MARTIN LUTHER KING, JR.:
THE LAST INTERVIEW

"Injustice anywhere is a threat to
justice everywhere."

$15.99 / $21.99 CAN
978-1-61219-616-9
ebook: 978-1-61219-617-6

CHRISTOPHER HITCHENS:
THE LAST INTERVIEW

"If someone says I'm doing this out of faith, I say,
Why don't you do it out of conviction?"

$15.99 / $20.99 CAN
978-1-61219-672-5
ebook: 978-1-61219-673-2

BILLIE HOLIDAY: THE LAST INTERVIEW
AND OTHER CONVERSATIONS

"What comes out is what I feel. I hate straight
singing."

$16.99 / $22.99 CAN
978-1-61219-674-9
ebook: 978-1-61219-675-6